LIVING
LABOR

LIVING
LABOR

Edited by Milena Hoegsberg and Cora Fisher

Sternberg Press

Contents

WORK

PLAY

Foreword

In his essay, "Light in Two Windows," the sociologist Nils Christie describes the conflicts that arose in Norway's transition from an agrarian fishing society to a technocracy. During this shift, the local school was, and remains, an important tool for preparing the population for the changing demands of working life, and a repository for the children and youth who no longer had a place in the chain of production. The poetic title of Christie's essay refers to an older fisherman's reminiscence of his childhood and the hard work of going out to sea with his father. If, upon their return from the day's work, they saw light in two windows at home, it meant that they had company (perhaps the itinerant teacher had come to visit). Having company meant that there would be no more work preparing the catch that evening.

Christie's essay was written for the anthology, *Phantom of Liberty*, which is being published in conjunction with the exhibition, "Learning for Life." Both the anthology and the exhibition explore early social democracy's focus on education as a form of liberation and as a vehicle for leveling differences in society.

Through a series of exhibitions and publications, Henie Onstad Kunstsenter (HOK) is examining and discussing the role of society, and by extension, the art institution. The exhibition "Arbeidstid" (a composite word that connotes the time spent working) explores structural changes on the continuum from formative education to adulthood work life.

"Learning for Life" and "Arbeidstid" are conceptually linked by the American artist Allan Sekula, whose work, *School is A Factory* (1978–80), shown in "Learning for Life" and reprinted in part here, is a stark critique of the role of the artist and art education under late capitalism. School is posited as a costly recruitment center and functions as a repository for youth, who would otherwise join the ranks of the unemployed. Art education obscures the reality that the vast majority of students will never even come close to pursuing a creative profession. Sekula's work points to another underlying interest connecting these two exhibitions: how school, through discipline and structure, primes us for work life and instills us with work ethic. This preparation is captured pointedly in Priscila Fernandes' *Naar de Speeltuin!* (2012), which documents KidZania, an international chain of theme parks for children operating in play areas at shopping centers. KidZania is designed as a staged workplace where children enact various professional and paid roles, for example, a retail salesperson, a fast food restaurant worker, or a surgeon. In a related work by Fernandes made the same year, *For A Better World*, we see adult workers who are trained in teamwork via free play. Both are significant with respect to the transition to a consumer-oriented society. Children's play has become instrumentalized and channeled into the recognition of and loyalty towards brand name goods, while adult workers participate in creative courses in order to increase their productivity.

"Arbeidstid" presents extant works as well as several new commissions that probe the issue of "work" as ideology. Due to its oil wealth and the state management, Norway currently enjoys a unique economic position. It has an actual workforce deficit, which results in increased work migration to the service sector, but also to the oil and energy sectors. In terms of private economy, Norwegians are not as hard hit as the rest of Europe. Despite the current disparities in economic security, the urgency to ask difficult questions about current conditions is undiminished. HOK's exhibitions, including "Arbeidstid," and its independent publications aim to examine the structural concerns that collectively impact us, now and into the future. "Arbeidstid" continues HOK's commitment to asking questions, alongside contemporary artists, about the time in which we are living.

Tone Hansen
Director, Henie Onstad Kunstsenter (HOK)

An exhibition about the time and space of labor

ARBEIDSTID

May 23–September 1, 2013

JESPER ALVÆR

DUNCAN CAMPBELL

MARIANNE FLOTRON

PAUL GRAHAM

TEHCHING HSIEH

RICHARD IBGHY & MARILOU LEMMENS

KLEINES POSTFORDISTISCHES DRAMA

SHARON LOCKHART

MTL {NITASHA DHILLON & AMIN HUSAIN}

MICHALA PALUDAN

OLIVIA PLENDER

ALLAN SEKULA & NOËL BURCH

Allan Sekula & Noël Burch, *The Forgotten Space*, 2010

Video (still), 112 min. Courtesy of Doc.Eye Film, Amsterdam.

Allan Sekula & Noël Burch, *The Forgotten Space*, 2010

Video (still), 112 min. Courtesy of Doc.Eye Film, Amsterdam.

Allan Sekula & Noël Burch, *The Forgotten Space*, 2010

Video (still), 112 min. Courtesy of Doc.Eye Film, Amsterdam.

Tehching Hsieh, *One Year Performance 1980–1981* Time Card

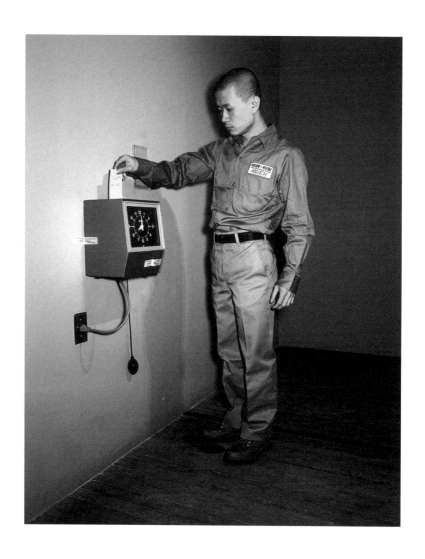

Tehching Hsieh, *One Year Performance 1980–1981* Punching the Time Clock

they are not even aware of all the structures they have internalized.

Marianne Flotron, *Work*, 2011

HDV (still), multi-channel installation. © Marianne Flotron. Produced by Kunsthalle Bern and Philippe Pirotte. Supported by Mondriaan Foundation Amsterdam; Carola und Günther Ketterer-Ertle, Bern; Rijksakademie van beeldende kunsten, Amsterdam.

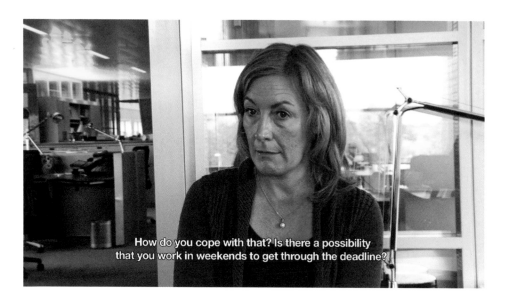

Marianne Flotron, *Work*, 2011

Installation view.

Duncan Campbell, *Make It New John*, 2009

Video (still), 50 min. © Duncan Campbell. Commissioned by the Film and Video

Umbrella, London; Chisenhale Gallery, London; Tramway, Glasgow; and

The Model, Sligo. Courtesy of Hotel, London.

Paul Graham, *Horse Poster, DHSS Office, Bristol*, 1984

#19 from the series *Beyond Caring*. Framed fuji crystal archive print, 88 × 107 cm. Edition of 5 plus 1AP; 2/5. © Paul Graham. Courtesy of Anthony Reynolds Gallery, London.

Paul Graham, *Mother and Baby, Highgate DHSS, North London*, 1984

#27 from the series *Beyond Caring*. Framed fuji crystal archive print, 88 × 107 cm. Edition of 5 plus 1AP; 2/5. © Paul Graham. Courtesy of Anthony Reynolds Gallery, London

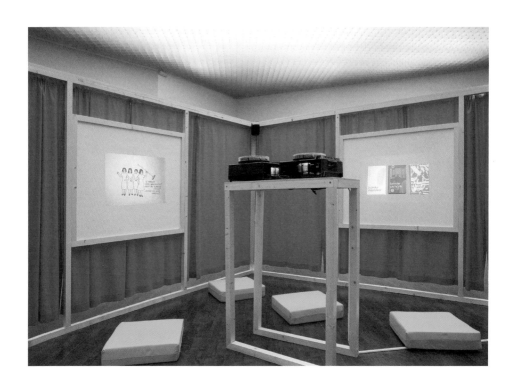

Michala Paludan, *Syklus*, 2013

Slide and sound installation. Produced by HOK with support from the Danish Arts Council.

Installation view.

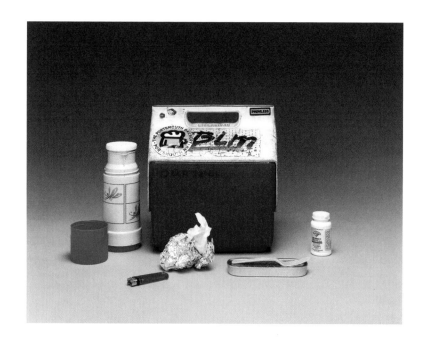

Sharon Lockhart, *Stanley "Tom" Durrell, Tinsmith*, 2008

Chromogenic print, 62.9 × 78.1 cm. © Sharon Lockhart. Courtesy of the artist;
neugerriemschneider, Berlin; Gladstone Gallery, New York and Brussels; and
Blum & Poe, Los Angeles.

Installation view.

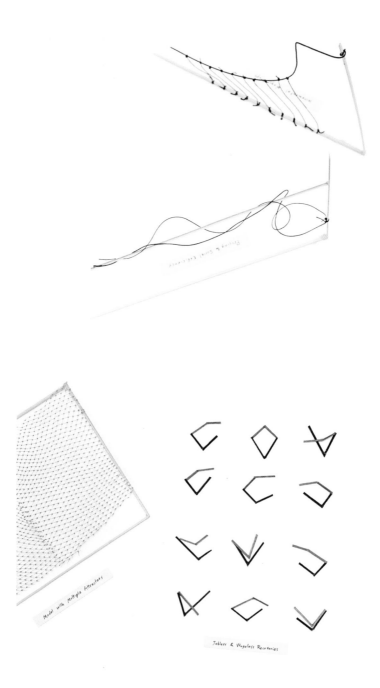

Richard Ibghy & Marilou Lemmens, *The Prophets*, 2013

Mixed media. Commissioned by HOK.

Employment Effects of Job Creation Schemes

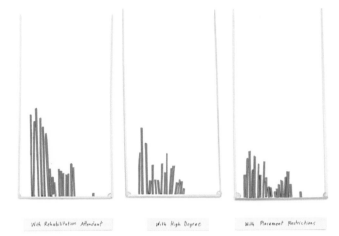

With Rehabilitation Attendant   With High Degree   With Placement Restrictions

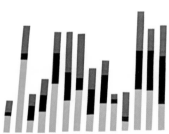

Credit Requirements for Interest Rate Swap Portfolios

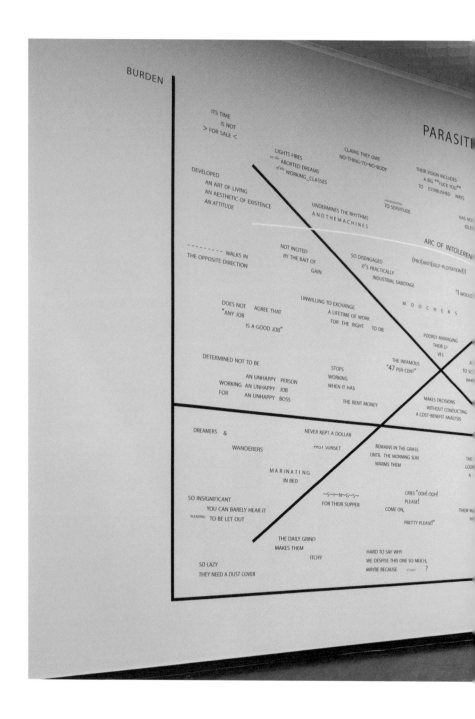

Richard Ibghy & Marilou Lemmens, *Parasites*, 2013

Vinyl on wall. Commissioned by HOK.

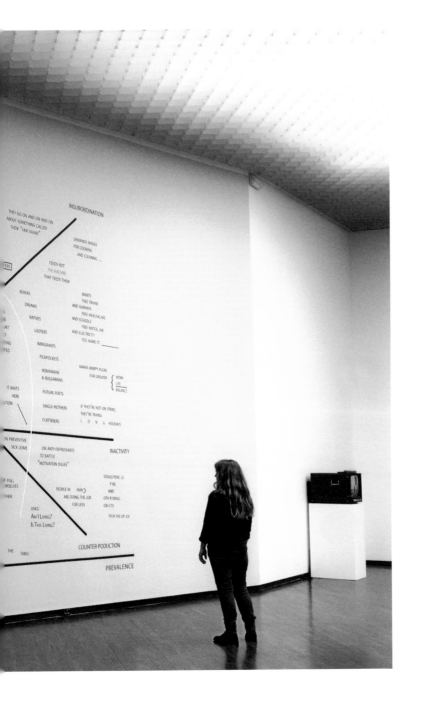

INSUBORDINATION

THEY GO ON AND ON AND ON
ABOUT SOMETHING CALLED
THEIR "FAIR SHARE"

DEMANDS WAGES
FOR COOKING
AND CLEANING ...

...TERS

FEEDS NOT
THE MACHINE
THAT FEEDS THEM

RONAS

WANTS
FREE TRAINS
AND SUBWAYS
FREE HEALTHCARE
AND SCHOOLS
FREE WATER, AIR
AND ELECTRICITY
YOU NAME IT:

DRUNKS

NATIVES

LOOTERS

IMMIGRANTS

PICKPOCKETS

MAKES WIMPY PLEAS
FOR GREATER

{ WORK
LIFE
BALANCE

ROMANIANS
& BULGARIANS

FUTURE POETS

SINGLE MOTHERS

IF THEY'RE NOT ON STRIKE,
THEY'RE TAKING

FLATTERERS

L O N G HOLIDAYS

IT WAITS
HERE

...TION

...ON PREVENTIVE
SICK LEAVE

ON ANTI-DEPRESSANTS
TO BATTLE
"MOTIVATION ISSUES"

INACTIVITY

...Y PULL
...MSELVES

...THER

PEOPLE IN VAIN
ARE DOING THE JOB
FOR LESS

STEALS PENC LS
P NS
AND
OTH R SMALL
OBJ C TS

ASKS:
AM I LIVING?
IS THIS LIVING?

FR M THE OF ICE

THE TABLE

COUNTER-PODUCTION

PREVALENCE

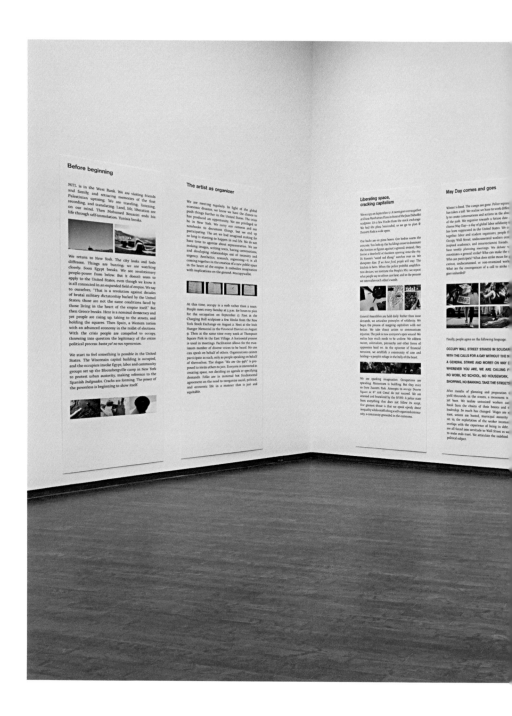

MTL (Nitasha Dhillon, Amin Husain & Friends)

#*OCCUPYWALLSTREET: A Possible Story* إنها ثورة حتّى النصر , 2013

Text on wall, felt pins. Commissioned by HOK.

...on debt and touch a nerve. The now
...dream is to get out of debt. Education
...ical debt, credit card debt, mortgage debt,
...ana. We meet people where they are at, where
...stance teaches our lives in the most imme-
...s. We gather and tell stories. The feeling of
...in weakness. The power of refusal—can't pay,
...The smell of the bills going up in smoke as
...y together. The images become actions and
...n. We perform our shared reality to break
...in, the shame, and the isolation, and build
...ty instead. We imagine debt as more than
...mes." We imagine debt as a placeholder for
...anizing system in its totality; debt as an
...of other oppressions; debt as a racist war
...debt as a distillation of neo-freedom. We
...other debts and other bonds to friends,
...community, rather than to the banks. Debts
...em immemorial histories of slavery and col-
...Debts that are both immeasurable and
...debts that mark our lives and relations in
...ways.

...and other racist, capitalist bullshit

The identity of the debtor gains traction, but primarily among middle-class white people. We know
that debt impacts poor communities of color the
hardest, from subprime mortgages to payday loans,
to urban austerity. Debt intersects with racialized
state violence on an everyday basis. All roads lead to
Wall Street, but they pass through the precinct, the
prison, and the morgue. As we reimagine resistance
to capitalism at an urban level, we think of those
killed by the NYPD, private security forces, and racist
vigilantes around the country.

AMADOU DIALLO   MANUEL DIAZ

SHANTEL DAVIS   RAMARLEY GRAHAM

SEAN BELL   TRAYVON MARTIN

OSCAR GRANT   KIMANI GRAY

...and so it goes.

Climate strike

Climate strikes back against Wall Street, and we all
get flooded. The banks are under water. The ocean
in the streets, block by block. The boardwalk is in
ruins. We convert churches into hubs for mutual
aid. There is a void left by the State. We do not hesi-
tate. We step in, we take the risk. It is a crisis and an
opportunity. We are reminded that "our struggle
against the concentration of wealth and power in
the hands of a few is also a struggle for life—and that
an obsession with growth and firing up a sputtering
economy misses the larger ecological questions
confronting the planet."

We offset the negligence of the city and the agencies
so everything won't fall further apart. A grey area
between emergency relief and political resistance; can
we pivot in that space? Can we align our responsibility
to act with what we are working toward? How do we
link climate to debt, to work, to sustainable living?

We go to Detroit with these questions.

It does not resemble a city

Detroit is a mythic wasteland of romantic ruins
and vacant space. This post-industrial picturesque
effaces those living and struggling in what used to
be the city. Capital and the state have withdrawn
from massive swathes of territory. Every square
inch is a Wall Street crime scene. In both its
devastation and possibility, Detroit is an outpost
from our collective future. Long-term struggles on
the ground throw everything into a new light:
our own cities, our own work, our own lives. Racial,
economic, and environmental justice understood
in a global context of empire, neo-liberalism, and
climate disaster. People thinking of revolutionary
time in decades and centuries, rather than in days
and months. Non-monetary economies; community-
based agriculture; work beyond jobs; education
beyond school; culture beyond art; life beyond
capitalism. In Detroit, we hear over and over:
how do we live?

• • •

Do you remember when they said
it was the end of history?

Do you remember when we couldn't imagine?

Do you remember when a borderless
world wasn't possible?

Do you remember when the crack
opened beneath our feet?

The liberated territories are coming.

حتى النصر
حتى النصر

kpD, *Kamera Läuft! (Rolling!)*, 2004

Video with sound, 32 min. Courtesy of kpD.

Time. The clock shows 8.

I'm sorry.

Jesper Alvær, *Konkret*, 2013

Video with sound (stills), 22 min. Commissioned by HOK. Courtesy of the artist.

Olivia Plender, *Self-direction Lounge*, 2013

Installation, mixed media. Commissioned by HOK.

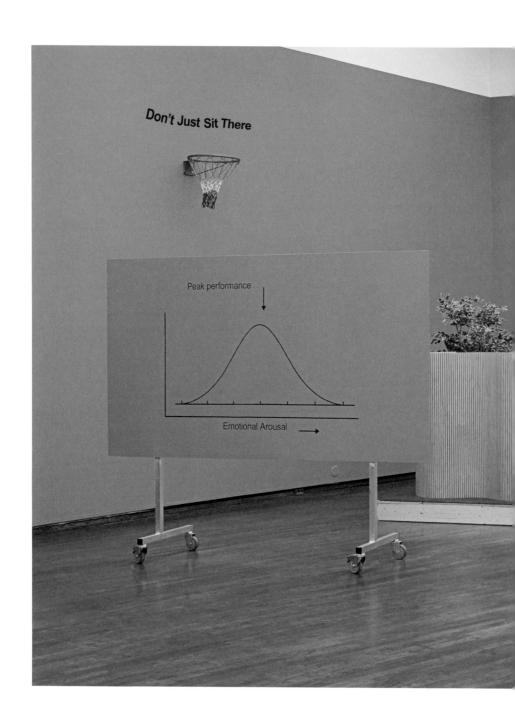

Olivia Plender, *Self-direction Lounge*, 2013

Installation, mixed media. Commissioned by HOK.

Introduction

IF NOT WORKERS, WHO WOULD WE BE?

Milena Hoegsberg

Just weeks ago (April 2013), the collapse of a factory building in
Savar, Bangladesh, made international news headlines. As the
death toll rose, questions of where to place the responsibility were
raised. The factory supplied the billion-dollar international garment
industry, and is one of many that makes up nearly eighty percent of
the country's export economy. Despite official warnings just days
before that the building was not up to code and was structurally
unsafe, workers were not told to evacuate prior to its fatal collapse.
The incident is a sobering reminder of the well-known flipside of
outsourcing production to developing countries with less strictly
enforced labor and environmental laws. And while emblematic
of a codependent global economy today, it will likely be soon
forgotten as the world's attention shifts elsewhere. Moreover, it
underscores that our global economic codependency makes it
so that we cannot separate our own working from that of others.
The developed countries feed a dominant work ideology through
capitalism, which sustains and worsens the working conditions
globally and across social classes.

Living Labor takes as its starting point this dominant ideology
of work and productivity propagated by today's global economic
system. It borrows its title from theorist Paolo Virno's term for the
post-Fordist working conditions, which enlist not only our working
hours but also those designated to think, dream, and imagine.[1]
In a collection of both reprinted and commissioned essays, this
publication explores "work" from different perspectives and
against the backdrop of the Scandinavian labor movement. Rather

than map conditions of global exploitation of which we are well aware, labor theorists Annette Kamp, Kathi Weeks, and Peter Fleming examine the slippage between life—leisure, as it were— and work. Of particular interest to the latter two thinkers is how we have internalized a work ethic, which compels us to fill our lives with work—that is, we work not because we have to, but because we feel we must.[2] While the total identification with work bespeaks a privileged position, it must be seen as intricately connected to its counterpart, the physical labor of those who work incessantly just to sustain themselves through what can barely be called a living wage.

In their strikingly apt accounts of the problems of work today, Weeks and Fleming point to the internalization of managerial logic, which prompts us to invest all of ourselves in work, and thus perform in work as a part of an elaborate self-actualization. More importantly, they make arguments for a need to formulate what *resistance* to work might look like in the future. Weeks proposes a shorter legal working day and a guaranteed basic income, but the conceptual framework she and Fleming put forward is more far reaching than that. The very question of what we *do* with more non-work time and who we would *be* if we were not workers, as Weeks has said eloquently, asks for a radical reimagination of the way we live.[3] Resistance is a process, which can start only with a critique of current conditions and then extend beyond them into an imaginary where the possibility of change might emerge.

Living Labor supplements and extends the thinking performed by the artworks in the exhibition "Arbeidstid" at Henie Onstad Kunstsenter (HOK).[4] The exhibition grew out of a dialogue with contemporary artists concerned with current economic and labor conditions, including their own. Artists generally hold a vulnerable position in today's economy. On one hand, they supply a system that privileges the creative information worker, capable of producing ideas and value (i.e., cultural capital).[5] On the other hand, artists are increasingly part of a growing assemblage of all types of "workers" who share the condition of precarity.[6] This overworked, underemployed, and underpaid group performs temporary work with no benefits, union representation, or security. For cultural producers, it is a vicious cycle: we work for free or for too little with the vague promise of a return on our career investment, which will allow us to start the slow repayment of personal debt from high education fees and living costs. In the art institution, the artist is all too often the only one not paid a wage for the work that they do. As professional identity has become fused with work to the extent that life is made subordinate to it, it seems even more absurd that our work should not be compensated. The artist represents the cultural producer *par excellence*, who has internalized the work ethic as a pillar of artistic purpose, and performs "not just the labor of the hand, but the labors of the head and heart."[7]

In "Arbeidstid" work is not fixed but performatively mediated. Rather than a clear notion of today's worker, "Arbeidstid" seeks to explore the temporal and spatial structures and the economic context from which this shifting paradigm of the worker emerges. The exhibition assumes the limitations—and to some degree the depletion—of documentary representations of the worker (*arbeiderbilder* in Norwegian), arguing instead for an activation of the terms and relationships between art practice, performance, work, and occupation. As Julia Bryan-Wilson points out in her essay "Occupational Realism," art is a privileged and exceptional form of work, and we should not lose sight of distinctions as we rethink the relationship between artistic and economic labor.

The current subordination of life to work is a wholesale liquidation of time traditionally tied to work, collapsing the distinction between time on and off the clock. As Annette Kamp notes in her essay published here, "New Concepts of Work and Time," the terminology associated with work and the workplace underscores the transition into a boundaryless work life. The Scandinavian word *arbeidstid* connotes time spent at work and, according to the Norwegian Working Environment Act, "the time a worker is available to his/her employer."[8] At the center of the exhibition hangs a Norwegian red banner from 1902 with the eight-hour workday movement's slogan of "eight hours labor, eight hours recreation, and eight hours rest." Labor historian Ole Martin Rønning reminds us in his essay that the official forty-hour workweek in effect today in Scandinavia is an achievement owed to the powerful labor movement, which, since the late 1800s, has fought to improve working conditions. The battle for fewer work hours was not just a claim for more time to recover from hard physical exertion, but also for time to use at one's own discretion. Even with a nominal lunch break, one had a clear sense of which hours belonged to oneself and which to the employer.

Sharon Lockhart's project *Lunch Break* (2009) is interesting in this regard. Working closely with a group of workers at the Bath Iron Works in Maine for over a year, she documents their non-productive moments, paying homage to the break during which the workers, as individuals, command the use of their own time in an otherwise rigid structure. In the film, she extends a single shot of a fifteen-minute break into eighty minutes. The break is taken in crammed hallways, where many prefer to sit, eat, do crossword puzzles, read the paper, listen to music, or look at family photos. The film is accompanied by a still-life series of individual lunch boxes, titled like portraits after the name of the workers and their official job titles. Alongside another series of photographs that capture pop-up independent food businesses within the industrial plant, the lunch boxes remind us of the technological and, with it, human obsolescence, as workplaces responding to global labor markets continue to become defunct. In a time of immaterial labor, the objects at the Bath Iron Works become material links to an industrial past and to a different temporal moment when the lunch break provided time to physically withdraw and let the mind drift. Today, potential mental breaks are too often filled, as we take lunch in front of our computers, or are on our smart phones. As Fleming argues, work occupies not just your working hours, but all your waking hours.

Packed lunch, 1886. This century old "madpakke" (a slice of dark bread with lard) was wrapped in the newspaper The Social Democrat and discovered between two walls in the 1980s where a worker presumably put it while on break.

Installation view with banner from the Workers Union "Fram," 1902.

Text front: 8 hours labor, 8 hours recreation, 8 hours rest.

Text back: The law's protection of the right to unionize.

© the Labor Movement Archives and Library of Oslo.

The increasing blur between time spent on and off the clock materializes in the spatial reconfigurations of workplace, as Lockhart's *Lunch Break* makes felt through obsolescence. The factory is also the troubled subject of *Make It New John* (2009), Duncan Campbell's film set in a car factory in Northern Ireland. The production of the DeLorian car, most familiar from its appearance as the time machine in *Back to the Future* (1985), was subsidized by the British Parliment in return for promising training and manual labor jobs at a time of severe economic downturn. Campbell creates a critical montage of documentary footage, contrasting the marketing rhetoric spun to sell the car, the circumstances of its production, and a staged interview of the workers (played by actors) after they were laid off when the factory went bankrupt. The film engages a specific moment when the unemployment rate was at a record high in Great Britain, during the 1980s global recession and under Margaret Thatcher's neoliberal policies.

Two color photographs by Paul Graham from the *Beyond Caring* series (1984) included in "Arbeidstid" document an unemployment office, just two years after the Delorian factory went bust. There is something universal about the spaces captured with a hidden camera, and the social identities they frame. Surprisingly, present-day food stamp and unemployment offices look similarly drab. Meanwhile, in countries with larger budgets for social services, such offices have been replaced with more colorful interiors suited for job centers, intended to encourage clients to stay optimistic and jolt them out of their current rut. However, the human condition of being unemployed—being reduced to a waiting number and a societal burden—is timeless. Here, one does not perform, but waits. The unemployed are suspended in a temporal limbo, as their social identity is stripped away and replaced with the stigmatization that attends the label of "unemployed." Both Campbell's and Graham's works take on enhanced meaning against the backdrop of the 2008 recession, the eurozone crisis, and the rise in especially young, educated people who may well be looking at dramatically diminished job prospects and possibly long term unemployment—a new so-called lost generation.[9]

The economic incentives and the drive for productivity behind work form the backbone of Richard Ibghy and Marilou Lemmens's large-scale graph *Parasites* (2013), which charts stereotypes of those seen as burdensome to productive society. It extends the idea of the social parasite from those out of work to those that refuse work as envisioned under the framework of capitalism's ethos of productivity and efficiency. As the artists argue, in the moral judgment of the parasite, what is often articulated is an antagonism toward a politics of pleasure and desire, as opposed to sacrifice and asceticism. The opposite of working is not being jobless. Rather, it is refusing to accept that work instrumentalizes all aspects of life, a more recent development.

In the second part of Ibghy and Lemmens's contribution to "Arbeidstid," a series of playful sculptures, handmade from ordinary household materials, render economic graphs into make-shift sculptures. Handwritten labels point to the economic models from which they are culled and aim to describe human behavior by analyzing the interactions between labor, consumption, produc-tion, savings, investments, credit, and other vectors. *The Prophets* (2013) translates the abstract language of economics into physical models, making apparent how often the language of finance, which purports to describe our lived economic reality, deliberately confounds through its abstraction.

In the context of Norway, it is of course ironic that the country, due to its oil reserves, has remained fairly immune to the crisis that has hit large parts of Europe and the United States. Yet, the number of short-term resident wage workers, primarily from Eastern European countries, is increasing as people find no future in their own countries and come to the wealthy North in search of a better life. Jesper Alvær's video work *Konkret* (2013), is based on conversations the artist had with forty-two day laborers he temporarily hired from an unemployment office in Oslo, special-izing in providing contracts for a few hours work, mostly limited to manual odd jobs, like painting walls, removing waste, assembling furniture and the like. In his video work, Alvær animates the drawings and notes the workers made during conversations he initiated with them about their work lives, the tasks at hand, and their participation in the making of a work of art. As Alvær recites words that they associate with work, a unique terminology arises that is both generic and granted meaning through individual associations.

The interest in the language of work courses through the exhibition, as seen in Ibghy and Lemmens's interrogation of social mores and finance-speak. In the large-scale installation commissioned for the exhibition, *Self-direction Lounge* (2013), Olivia Plender appropriates language linked to corporate culture and vocabulary for measuring economic and work performance. Plender created different kinds of work zones, divided by screens, which emphasize the set-like quality of flexible and open offices you might find today both in Norway and beyond. These lifestyle-oriented working environments aim to make it more "fun" to be at work, boost your creativity and performance, and reduce the urge to "check-out." While visually attractive and inviting, Plender's installation feels decidedly constructed and deliberately made to feel just enough like a stage to disallow a full and uncritical immersion. The work points to the demands placed on workers to be entrepreneurial and to self-actualize through their jobs, with the inherent risk of instrumentalizing all aspects of their subjectivity. Visitors are invited to use the space and, in doing so, willingly participate in the production of values that the work of art generates.

Marianne Flotron's four-channel video *Work* (2011), like Plender's *Self-direction Lounge*, addresses the freedoms gained in the flexible workplace, freedoms which rely on the prediction of behavioral patterns of workers. Flotron's work is based on conversations with employees at a Dutch insurance company. Carefully screened prior to being hired, each worker has already proved they possess the psychological makeup necessary to perform well in a flexible work environment that requires self-management. As the video makes clear, the internalization of the managerial voice and the complete alignment of the firm's goals and the employee's inner desires or ambitions lead to voluntary self-exploitation that constitutes a source of stress.

In the quest to find agency and resist the current pressures of work, language becomes a productive field to shift thought. Michala Paludan's installation *Syklus* ("cycle") (2013), also commissioned for this exhibition, ventriloquizes the voices of different Danish women from the 1970s interviewed about their work and private lives. Paludan's installation is based on the organizational structures of *basisgrupper* (basis groups). In Scandinavia, these small, informal, and inclusive groups of women were seen as key frameworks to develop a collective politics, rooted firmly in the experiences and needs of women. The sound-track of voices supplement slide images of women taken from the labor movement archives in Oslo and Copenhagen. These images testify to what has been achieved over the past decades and to the inequalities that remain. The theatrical structure of the installation, with curtains draped around a framed room, is both public and private. It mimics the organizational structure of *basisgrupper*, insisting on the feminist claim that the personal is political.

MTL also speaks to a space of active resistance through a claiming of space and a renegotiation of language. The group's narrative text and image work #*Occupywallstreet: A Possible Story* إنها لثورة حتى النصر (2013), weaves in and out of different voices. MTL calls attention to Occupy's distinctive heterogeneity as a composite community, a multidirectional protest movement and a political platform, asking, "how do we live?" Their text in the exhibition ties labor to issues of climate-change politics, resistance move-ments in and out of the United States, economic inequality, and debt. It asserts that any imagination of a different future must start on the ground with conversations and collaboration. Paradoxically, they capture both the strength of Occupy as a platform, but also what might be its failure: that it rejects making directed political demands—the very thing that granted the labor movement power—in the attempt to give voice to the concerns of people of various communities. These artists posit a speculative utopianism mobilized within a transient organizational structure as they ask, "how can we pivot in that space?" and point again to the performative possibilities of occupation.

As MTL reminds us, what characterizes this moment is the need to probe work as a system and as a way of life, not just as profession. They allow us to formulate new imaginaries, other possibilities beyond those proscribed by hegemonic discourse. Refusal can, as Kathi Weeks argues, "make time and open spaces—both physical and conceptual—within which to construct alternatives."[10] What precedes resistance to the status quo and change is a willingness to imagine that things can be different.

Notes

1 The genealogy of the term also refers to Marxist theory, where living labor is the human labor power that, when joined with production, is transformed into capital to generate new value and use value. In the context of this book, living labor assumes the emotional, affective, and immaterial qualities of working life—the understanding that we are increasingly living out labor at the expense of other dimensions of existence.

2 Kathi Weeks, *The Problem with Work: Feminism, Marxism, Antiwork Politics, and Postwork Imaginaries* (Durham: Duke University Press, 2011), chapter 1.

3 Kathi Weeks, "Imagining Non-Work," Periscope, (March 28, 2013,) http://www. socialtextjournal.org/periscope/2013/03/ imagining-non-work.php.

4 *Living Labor* is in a sense a parallel production and includes many images of works not included in the exhibition as well as two visual essays by Michala Paludan and Olivia Plender & Hester Reeves.

5 For a shortlist of books and exhibition catalogues that focus on labor's relation to the field of art, see: Helen Molesworth, ed., *Work Ethic* (Baltimore: Baltimore Museum of Art, 2003); Julieta Aranda, Anton Vidokle, Brian Kuan Wood, eds., *Are You Working Too Much?: Post-Fordism, Precarity, and the Labor of Art* (Berlin: Sternberg Press, 2011); Cecilia Widenheim et al., eds., *Work, Work, Work: A Reader on Art and Labor* (Berlin: Sternberg Press, 2012); Sønke Gau, Katharina Schlieben, eds., *Work to do!: Self-Organisation in Precarious Working Conditions* (Nuremberg: Verlag

für Moderne Kunst, 2009); Silvia Eiblmayr, Christiane Erharter et al., eds., *At Your Service: Art and Labour* (Salzburg: Fotohof, 2012); Silvia Eiblmayr, Katy Deepwell, eds., *Arbeit* (Frankfurt am Main: Revolver, 2005). See also exhibitions: "I Can't Work Like This" (Casco– Office for Art, Design and Theory, NL, 2012); "All I Can See is the Management" (Gasworks, EN, 2011); Atelier Europa (Munich Kunstver- ein, DE, 2004)

6 Julia Bryan-Wilson, "Occupational Realism," 119.

7 Weeks, *Problem with Work*, 69.

8 Arbeidsmiljølovens 10–1 "den tid arbeids- taker står til disposisjon for arbeidsgiver."

9 Rising unemployment in the United States and in large parts of Europe has been well documented. Nearly a quarter of global youth are "economically inactive" (not in job, training, or education.) See, for example, David Jolly, "U.N. Agency Warns of Rising Unemployment," *New York Times*, January 21, 2013.

10 Weeks, *Problem with Work*, 100.

LABOR MOVEMENT ARCHIVES —MORE THAN HISTORICALLY RELEVANT?

Ole Martin Rønning

It is possible to envision the history of the labor movement in
Norway as analogous to a lifespan. Conception occurred at the
end of the 1800s, and early childhood lasted up to 1918. Then
came the radical "new direction" with its revolutionary politics.
The 1920s and first half of the 1930s were characterized by social
upheaval and class struggles—the Norwegian labor movement's
restless and rebellious adolescence. The movement reached
maturity with control of the government in 1935, but was then
forced underground, exiled by the Nazi regime during the Second
World War. The ensuing years, however, from 1945 to 1981 came to
be its "golden age," its adulthood. By the 1980s, aging and decline
began to set in. The labor movement's sustaining ideological
foundations of social solidarity, a regulated economy, and welfare
reforms for the good of all seemed to be losing sway. A conservative wave—economic neoliberalism combined with deregulation of
financial institutions, privatization, and competitive outsourcing
of the public sector services, as well as the call for increased
individual freedom—began to erode the traditional model of
social administration from the labor movement's golden age.
The latter half of the 1990s saw an immense rise in prosperity with
the exploitation of oil and natural gas deposits on the Norwegian
continental shelf. One might be tempted to believe that the labor
movement has now arrived at its final resting place, inasmuch
as Norway has seemingly become a bourgeois nation living on
an island of riches, immune to the economic crisis which plagues
the rest of Europe today. Or, does the movement live on in
new guises?

The Labor Movement Archives and Library

The Labor Movement Archives and Library (in Norwegian, *Arbeider-bevegelsens arkiv og bibliotek* or *Arbark*) was established in the fall of 1908, a joint undertaking of the Norwegian Labor Party and the Norwegian Confederation of Trade Unions, with the aim of collecting and preserving all types of documentation from the labor movement and thereby becoming a source of reliable information about the movement's history and activities. Establishing a repository of knowledge and disseminating this knowledge was a necessary means of promoting and furthering the working class' political and economic interests. The liberation of the working class also had a cultural aspect, educating workers in how to shape their daily lives and participate in the steering of society. Here the establishment of the archive served in training, development, and perhaps satisfying a desire to account for progress during the labor movement's historic march towards its goal: political and social power.

Reconstructing the past on a foundation of more than just hearsay, individual recollection, and experience requires source material passed on by those involved. And among the diversity of material, what is contained in an archive has a unique status. If archival material is safeguarded and described in accordance with archival science and methodology, it assumes a degree of authenticity as documentation. Today there are three main professional principles that guide the administration of an archive: preserve sources of the archive creator's activity, preserve material for future research, and preserve broad and comprehensive social documentation.

From the time that the Labor Party took control of the government in 1935—facilitated by support from the Farmer's Party—the labor movement was dominant in setting the terms for the development of modern Norway. In the new national consensus that emerged with the end of the Nazi occupation in 1945, the social democratic leaning within the labor movement prevailed in the reconstruction of the country. In the ensuing twenty years, governments stemming

Poster, The Norwegian Labor Party (Det norske Arbeiderparti),

Elections (Stortingsvalget), 1933. Design: Erling Nielsen.

© the Labor Movement Archives and Library of Oslo.

from the Labor Party led the country, the conservative parties were left on the sidelines, and the communists were marginalized. During these years, the character of the social democratic labor movement evolved from having been an opposition movement bent on gaining power to representing the instrument of power itself.

What were the consequences of this shift for the Labor Movement Archives and Library? Its collections acquired new content. What had begun as a documentation project with the aim of safeguarding what was produced by a movement in political opposition, an effort to maintain a collective memory and forestall its erasure over the course of time, gradually turned into a documentation of the exercise of power. The personal archives of Labor Party prime ministers, cabinet ministers, and powerful party secretaries filled the archive's shelves. The central bureaucracy of the organized labor movement, both in the Norwegian Confederation of Trade Unions and the individual labor unions, produced comprehensive archives from participation in the formation of what is known as "the Norwegian model": the tripartite cooperation between the state, employer's organizations, and organized labor.

Yet the archive's original intentions have also been maintained. That is to say, not only the exercises of power, but also grass roots activities continue to be documented. And unlike corresponding archives in other countries (Finland, for example), the Labor Movement Archives and Library hosts the entire political left wing in Norway; the Norwegian Communist Party, the Socialist People's Party (now the Socialist Left Party), and the Maoists of the Worker's Communist Party have all placed their archives here.

Causes, Before and Now

Industrialization involved a comprehensive exploitation of the new industrial proletariat. The working day was twelve-hours long or longer. There was little time left over for life outside the workplace.

Since its establishment in 1889, the Socialist International (SI) has had the eight-hour workday as its leading cause. The issue came to be associated with May Day demonstrations in all parts of the world, and in Norway a united labor movement became galvanized around the demand for shorter working hours. When the Norwegian labor movement launched an offensive in 1918 for the adoption of the eight-hour workday, their effort occurred within a larger international context of direct actions. The Bolsheviks' October Revolution in Russia the previous year had inspired the creation of workers' councils in Norway as well. The workers' councils would lead the labor movement's struggles against commodities and food shortages, yet they also had revolutionary potential as alternative and non-parliamentary power structures. Many believed the workers' councils would be able, by means of demonstrations or general strikes, to seize power. It was an ambitious goal. As a first step, in March 1918 a national assembly of the workers' councils sanctioned a motion for workers to, by their own volition, institute or "assume" the eight-hour workday as of May 2. Throughout most of the country the action was a fiasco, and the workers' council movement more or less collapsed.

Nevertheless, the eight-hour workday was realized in 1919. Both the conservative government and employers feared the possible consequences of large scale workers' action. There was a desire to support the moderate agents within the labor movement, and as an accommodation to them, one that would give workers greater confidence in the existing social system, the government estab-lished the eight-hour workday in labor law. Almost one hundred years later, memorabilia from the struggle for the eight-hour day still exists in the form of writings, pamphlets, newspaper clippings, and other written contemporary documents, banners with revolu-tionary slogans, photographs, and written personal recollections.

Collective social movements with ambitions of changing condi-tions in society continue to exist, although today such movements are usually network oriented, and the international perspective is particularly important. Compared with the labor movement's struggle a century ago, contemporary social movements have changed in many ways. Being rooted in a particular social class is less important now, and causes are usually more ideologically or identity oriented, as opposed to the interests-oriented and material objectives of previous eras. The organizational arrangement of movements has changed as well, from formal hierarchies to flatter, more transient structures. The adversary remains the same—capitalism—but its character has changed. The consequences of globalized capitalism are giving rise to new forms of resistance.

Does the Labor Movement Archives and Library have any other function today than bearing testimony to a bygone era, a struggle waged under entirely different circumstances? Or serving as a monument to a kind of mythical social democratic ideal society said to have existed in Scandinavia back in the 1960s? A contributor of selected glossy images trotted out for banquet speeches? Regardless, the history of the labor movement's struggles is preserved for posterity, and we have to believe that being able to communicate information about past battles waged and the shape of those battles can serve as an inspiration. But the most important memorial is perhaps that the victories won were a result of collective action. The labor movement's solidarity and potential threat to the status quo impelled those changes. The lesson learned is that it takes both solidarity and power to change society.

The anti-globalization movement and, in recent years, the Occupy movement have become significant social movements. Compared with the labor movement, these new movements are quite different and problematic. After Arab Spring, contemporary revolutionary movements, network and Internet-based, have a transient organizational character. Their ambitions of direct democracy, with general assemblies and consensus-based decision-making, constitute a contrast to the organized labor movement's formal and hierarchical structures. The archival material is different—resolution protocols have been replaced by web pages. Organization transpires via cellphone text messaging. The Norwegian workforce is also in flux. Unlike the situation in other Scandinavian countries,

Rail strike, mass meeting at Youngstorget, Oslo, after

the big demonstration, Saturday, December 4, 1920.

there is currently high demand for labor in Norway, a demand being met by immigration. In 2011 over 26,000 immigrant workers came to Norway. There were also, at the end of the same year, 71,000 wage earners registered as short-term residents (less than six months). Setting aside other Scandinavians, the majority of these immigrant workers come from the Eastern European countries admitted to the EU in 2004, predominantly Poland and Lithuania. Few are union organized, thus they have no form of collective representation and are often in a vulnerable position. Compared to ordinary workers in Norway, migrating workers' rights are far less secure. Additionally, the fact that this new proletariat in the Norwegian workforce is largely unorganized, unaffiliated with any union, also impedes its being documented through the means the Labor Movement Archive and Library has at its disposal today. The Archive primarily documents movements, or perhaps more precisely organizations, as well as the prospective activities of individuals within these organizations.

A major concern of the Labor Movement Archives and Library is capturing and recording current social movements. Yet, paradoxically, it has become more difficult to document causes today than it was a century ago. Communication has taken other more elusive, intangible forms. Information on websites can vanish with a keystroke. If the archive is to continue to have relevance as a repository of documentation, it is obliged to adapt to the new forms of communication. More than just an objective, this is a necessity.

References / Sources

Knut Einar Eriksen, Solveig Halvorsen, and

Einar A. Terjesen, "Arbeiderbevegelsens arkiv

og bibliotek gjennom 100 år," *Arbeiderhistorie*

(2008): 7–69.

Knut Kjeldstadli, "Kollektive bevegelser," in

Historier om motstand: Kollektive bevegelser

i det 20. århundret, ed. Idar Helle,

Knut Kjeldstadli, and Jardar Sørvoll

(Oslo: Abstrakt forlag, 2010), 13–32.

Finn Olstad, *Med knyttet neve, LOs historie*

1899–1935 (Oslo: Pax, 2009).

Gudmund Valderhaug, *Fotnote eller tekst?*

Arkiv og arkivarar i det 21. hundreåret

(Oslo: ABM-Media, 2011).

"Innvandrere etter innvandringsgrunn, 1. januar

2012," August 30, 2012, http://www.ssb.no/

emner/02/01/10/innvgrunn/.

"Sysselsatte på korttidsopphold, 2011, 4.

kvartal," June 25, 2012, http://www.ssb.no/

emner/06/01/kortsys/.

LETTER TO TATE BRITAIN

Ann Gallagher
Head of Collections (British Art)
Tate Britain
Millbank
London SW1P 4RG
—

Olivia Plender and Hester Reeve
The Emily Davison Lodge
c/o The Women's Library
London Metropolitan University
25 Old Castle Street
London E1 7NT

May 13, 2010

Dear Ann Gallagher,

This letter is a request for an appointment to discuss the importance of Tate Britain collecting the work of the British artist Sylvia Pankhurst (1882–1960) and promoting her significance to the nation. We both have established art careers and also lecture in the practice and theory of Fine Art (Chelsea School of Art and Sheffield Hallam University) and this letter, along with the reinstatement of the Emily Davidson Lodge, arises out of research for a commissioned exhibition hosted by the Women's Library (*Out of the Archives* curated by Anna Colin May to October 2010).

We feel it only right to present the grounds for such a request:

Sylvia Pankhurst's name is well documented within social and political history on account of her celebrated mother and family's campaign for female suffrage via the establishment of the WSPU (Women's Social & Political Union) in 1903. But less celebrated is how, aside from being a leading figure of the campaign to win women the vote in this country, Sylvia Pankhurst was also a highly skilled, versatile and pioneering artist in her own right. In our recent research into her work, we are saddened by the lack of recognition accorded her as an artist and the ongoing pervasive attitudes within society and the arts that such an omission might stand for. Tate Britain currently has no works by Sylvia Pankhurst in the collection and seems to have omitted specific recognition of any feminist impact upon art history in its thematic arrangements of British art 1700 to present date despite counter culture and rebel voices having always played a serious role in the formation of British culture.

Sylvia Pankhurst's practice ranged from drawing to painting, from fine art to craft, suffragette propaganda, banner and movement identity design to public speaking, writing and political activism. In our time, when any singular narrative of the traditional argument of art versus life has expanded beyond any neat categorisation of either, the practice of Sylvia Pankhurst forms the basis for renewed discussion into arts relationship to "change"—do we in the art world know how to value "deeds not words" in 2010?

The suffragette insistence on Deeds not Words, carried through seventy years later to the women's lib claim that The Personal is the Political, seems ready for a third stage of reappraisal in the ongoing fight to realise equality for women and the representation of female artists within the canon of art history.

Some further historical facts to back up our proposal to accord Sylvia Pankhurst her due place in British art history:

She studied at Manchester Municipal School of Art and then went on to win a scholarship at the Royal College of Art (she was later to challenge them on their prejudice against women artists). Her practice expanded upon becoming a WSPU leader; she designed banners and logos (most notably the "angel of freedom" which featured on badges, tea pots and the front page of *Votes For Women*, the suffragette newspaper). It is claimed that this is the first instance of a campaigning organisation deliberately using design and colour to present an "identity." Of further note is her *Holloway Broach* (1909), a silver design incorporating the portcullis and arrowhead of freedom which was awarded to WSPU suffragettes who had been imprisoned for their actions and the huge twenty-foot banners she designed for the famous fundraising Suffragette Exhibition at the Princes Skating Rink in 1909.

WSPU brooch designed by Sylvia Pankhurst, 1909, awarded to released WSPU prisoners. Drawing by Hester Reeve, ink on paper, 2010. Courtesy of the artist.

OLIVIA PLENDER AND HESTER REEVE

An active militant, Sylvia Pankhurst was involved in some of the key moments of the WSPU campaign. Before the avantgardes had ripped up their first canvas, she was one of the first to attack an artwork, recognising its status as a symbol of patriarchal power and "the secret idol of capitalism." Other artists of the time acknowledged the power of these actions, for example Wyndam Lewis (founder of the British Vorticist movement) gave the movement his blessing in the publication *Blast*, with the words: "We admire your energy. You and artists are the only things…left in England with a little life left in them."

Left to right: Emily Davison, Sylvia Pankhurst displaying a wooden model of her Holloway Prison Emblem, Christabel Pankhurst and Emmeline Pethick Lawrence in a suffragette procession, 1910. Photo: David Mitchell. Courtesy of Richard Pankhurst.

Sylvia Pankhurst was imprisoned many times for her actions. While in Holloway she went on a hunger strike alongside other suffragettes, suffered force-feeding and yet also made sketches of prison life so she could publicise the adverse conditions to the outside world. The Penal Reform Union was in fact formed at one of the breakfast-welcomes held upon her release from jail. She also produced one of the first historical overviews of the campaign, *The Suffragette: The History of the Women's Militant Suffragette Movement 1905–10,* published in 1911 and then later in 1931 one of the most notable accounts in existence, *The Suffragette Movement.*

Aside from the art and activism, Sylvia Pankhurst's particular contribution to the historical force of the suffragette movement was to encourage working women and the poor to take power (depicting a mill woman and a washer woman, for example, on the suffragette members card that she designed in 1905). Indeed, her own criticism of the WSPU was that it was too bourgeois and in 1913, she officially broke ties and founded the East London Federation of Suffragettes (which later became the Workers' Socialist Federation). Here she worked with all strata of society and allowed men to join in the cause:

"I was looking to the future; I wanted to rouse these women of the submerged mass to be, not merely an argument of more fortunate people, but to be fighters on their own account, despising mere platitudes and catch-cries, revolting against the hideous conditions about them, demanding for themselves and their families a full share in the benefits of civilisation and progress." (*The Suffragette Movement,* 416-7)

Pankhurst always displayed a heightened consciousness about

Womens' Social and Political Union (WSPU) badge, showing the Angel of Freedom logo, design by Sylvia Pankhurst 1909. Drawing by Hester Reeve, ink on paper, 2010. Courtesy of the artist.

the complexities of practicing as an artist and yet simultaneously wishing to be of service to society. She wanted to put her art at the service of the poor and yet to fund herself as an artist meant dependence on bourgeois patrons:

...it was worthwhile to fight one's individual struggle ...to make one's way as an artist, to bring out of oneself the best possible, and to induce the world to accept one's creations, and give one in return ones' daily bread, when all the time the real struggles to better the world for humanity demand another service. (Myself When Young, by Famous Women of Today, 284)

These conflicts provide a radical backdrop to her "representational" works created when she toured the country making drawings of working-class women in their various places of labour. Some commentators have claimed that a crucial turning point in the Liberal PM Lord Asquith's antipathy for the women's vote was when he realised, through Sylvia Pankhurst's work and campaigning, just how many British women constituted the nation's workforce. For all the passion dedicated to political and social reform, Pankhurst never faltered to declare that art was her "chosen mission which gave satisfaction and pleasure found in nothing else." (The Suffragette Movement, p 428)

Pankhurst continued throughout her life to engage with art and politics. She later joined the pan-African movement and fought for the independence of Ethiopia, against Mussolini. She subsequently settled there and is still recognised today by the Ethiopian art world as a serious cultural figure.

We bring these biographical facts to your attention, not just to impress upon you Sylvia Pankhurst's importance but to again link such a significant life work to the advent of British modern art. She stands as a radical forerunner to the later aims of the European avant-garde, indeed this fact can be backed up by the Italian Futurist Marinetti's claim that: "In this campaign for liberation, our best allies are the suffragettes." (from *Le Futurisme*, 1911).

For all of the above, we have nonetheless found no instances of Sylvia Pankhurst being included in books on the relation between art and radical politics and rarely does one find books dedicated to her art practice, the Women's Library in London excepting. Ultimately, the great radical nature of her achievement lies in the combination of art and activism. Like her fellow militant suffragettes, Sylvia Pankhurst did not just fight for the vote; she fought for the creation of new forms of political life. Having said, "I would like to be remembered as a citizen of the world," she fought for freedom not only for women in Britain but also for women around the globe. Ironically she remains an uncelebrated figure within British art despite contemporary expanded definitions of art and interest in its social agency.

In view of the above, we would very much appreciate an occasion to discuss Tate Britain making specific display of Sylvia Pankhurst's work and the promotion of her remarkable practice to the British public.

Thank you for your consideration, we look forward to meeting you.

Yours sincerely,

Olivia Plender and Hester Reeve

ARBEIDERBILDER

Will Bradley

Edvard Munch's famous painting *Workers in the Snow* (1910) is
focused on one central figure, larger than life and looking directly
at the viewer. It is hard to say for sure what is on his mind, but his
expression is not particularly friendly. Behind him are many others,
less defined but very present, some lined up behind him, others in
the distance still working, sketched in monochrome or silhouette.
Munch is reaching for an archetypal image, an individual figure
picked out from the working masses who nonetheless is interchangeable with any of his comrades; not because he has no
individuality but exactly because all share this same quality
of being individuals pressed into a common social form. These
people are workers, but the leading figures are not working, simply
looking back at us. This extension of their identity beyond the
strict confines of their labor is surely an intentional representation
of class consciousness, the awareness of strength gained,
paradoxically, from an enforced unity, and it is easy to imagine
that the shovels and pickaxes they carry could become weapons
in some future confrontation.

Munch's existing writing has little to say about his personal
politics, aside from a later enthusiasm for art as public good rather
than private treasure, but the few clues that survive point in a
clear direction. *The Scream* was first reproduced next to an article
campaigning for the eight-hour workday, and a series of rough
drawings in one of Munch's sketchbooks from around 1908 give
further substance to an interpretation of *Workers in the Snow*
as a confrontational image. A sketch of one of his neighbors in

Kragerø is undoubtedly the model for the central figure, and there is evidence to suggest that this same neighbor was an active anarcho-syndicalist organizer. What is certain is that, later in the same sketchbook, we see Munch experimenting with the iconic imagery of the workers' movement of the time, a disembodied arm wielding a hammer, in front of a crowd that seems to represent Christiania's bohemian bourgeoisie.

A decade later, in the years around 1920, Munch returned to the subject of labor and made many rough sketches, drawings, and watercolors of manual workers. These have been rarely exhibited. Some documented the construction of his studio at Ekeli in Oslo, but many of these works on paper were clearly made in various other locations around the city. Unusually for Munch, these often appear to be street sketches or watercolors painted on location. In their vivid and unorthodox, but harmonious coloring; their integration of figure and ground even in half-sketched scenes; their lightness of touch and flattened perspective, the watercolors, in particular, have a utopian quality. It is certainly possible to imagine that these pictures aspire to show manual labor as beautiful, not in itself but as part of a social whole in which it plays a central part.

Do these shifts in the treatment of the subject represent Munch's intellectual conversion from bohemian to anarchist to believer in the virtues of the new social democracy? Beyond the work itself, the evidence of his convictions is rare and unconfirmed, but one obvious reading is that the confrontational attitude of the Kragerø period has given way to an image of integration and even optimism. Certainly, there is a sense that the condition of the working class in Norway is a problem that might be solved, and the competing interpretation—that Munch has resigned from political engagement to contemplate life's rich tapestry from a position of aesthetic disinterest—is hard to sustain. Further evidence that Munch found sufficient grounds for faith in the state comes in 1928, when he began working on a series of murals for the proposed new Oslo City Hall.

In contrast to the allegorical approach of many of the other artists commissioned to decorate the City Hall's interior, Munch planned to depict and celebrate the labor involved in the construction of the building itself. Interruptions of war and occupation meant that the City Hall was not completed until 1950 and Munch, having died in 1944, was in no position to finish the work he had started. Still, it seems unlikely that his proposed paintings could have represented more than a brief moment of clarity among the fantastic profusion of competing, contradictory, muralized origin myths of the Norwegian state in the extraordinary and unique *gesamtkunstwerk* of the building's public interior spaces.

Externally, City Hall represents an unfortunate architectural victory in the struggle to impose formal unity on a patchwork of competing ideological demands: a faux-medieval/Viking hall elaborated on Arts and Crafts principles, wearing an Art Deco factory skin, and burdened with double towers that seem to simultaneously proclaim and disavow the unity of Church and State, both comfortingly nondescript and disconcertingly totalitarian. Still, though it lacks Munch's intended paintings of the workers that built it, the design has one key contribution to make to the public depiction of labor. On the eastern side, at street level, a sculptural relief breaks the vast expanse of brickwork. A solid-looking bourgeois fellow in a top hat, carved in stone, larger than life and raised up from the ground, stands arm in arm with a confident-looking woman in fancy clothes. It is only when you come closer that you realize that the woman is also clandestinely holding the hand of another man—clearly, by his clothing, a member of the lower classes—who is hidden around the corner of the building.

This is *Albertine*, a sculpture by Alfred Seland from the novel of the same name by Christian Krohg, a story of young girls driven to prostitution by poverty. It is obviously an aside, a whispered joke in the context of otherwise serious proceedings. But still it is right there, built into the skin of an edifice conceived to represent modern Norway in brick and stone, and it is hard avoid reading it alongside the many other allegorical works that decorate the City Hall. If, on the surface, it is an everyday story of prostitute, pimp, and john, we can still easily imagine that the woman also represents the young social democratic state, whose heart belongs to the working class, but whose economic future depends on the unloving embrace of capitalism.

By the time City Hall was completed, the first, idealistic phase of the development of modern Oslo was also almost complete. Beginning in the early 1920s, this phase was characterized by strong regulation with a social democratic character, coupled with conservative classicist architecture that expanded the city to the north and east. What followed was a centrally-planned, hybrid parochial/ultra-modernist phase—far from unique in northern Europe—that produced, among other more worthwhile things, the housing developments most often referred to as Stalin blocks, and a disruptive and dysfunctional urban highway system.

Since the end of the 1980s there has been a gradual progression to a loosely regulated public/private partnership model that has enabled new suburban expansion, substandard infill development, and a series of grand political projects free from strict architectural or social demands. The latest phase has been evolving over the last two decades, under the banner of the Fjord City, and encompasses the paradigmatic post-industrial redevelopment of the city's waterfront. First shipbuilding, then the related shipping industry services, and then the urban port itself have been downsized and relocated as land value and rents have been reappraised in the light of the restructuring Norwegian economy.

In their place is a sequence of developments that self-consciously contribute to the construction of the contemporary image of the city: Landmark cultural buildings; vast new corporate HQs out on Fornebu; a maze of luxury apartments and high-end chain restaurants along the waterfront that can turn lifelong Oslo residents into lonely tourists; the Barcode development of corporate financial buildings, designed to present a seamless image of a city dedicated to commerce, but only from a virtual viewpoint hovering somewhere out above the fjord.

Of course there is no Oslo Eden that these developments despoil. If City Hall remains the anomalous focus of the Fjord City's waterfront arc, it should be remembered that it was itself a gentrification project, built on land freed by slum clearance. The question here is more specific: if Munch aspires to paint the builders of the City Hall, then, in all of this construction, what happened to the public representation of labor? Even outside the City Hall, postwar Oslo was dotted with public monuments to the working class; Per Palle Storm's sculptures on Akerbrygge and Youngstorget, or Erling Saatvedt's *Washday* at Enerhaugen are typical examples.

One explanation might be that a technological shift in the means of architectural construction and a political withdrawal from public space finally replaced the blind end walls and classical squares, open passages and grand atria of earlier designs with glass curtain walls and downsized, secure entranceways. Carl Nesjar's collaborations with Picasso on the concrete reliefs that decorate Norway's government buildings then appear not as social democratic celebrations but as elegies for the end of an era, an end that is definitively marked by Guttorm Guttormsgaard's ceramic reanimation of Rolf Nesch's prints on the vast brick facade of Oslo Spektrum.

Following a well-established historical line of Marxist art criticism, it could of course also be argued that as the economic basis of Norwegian society has shifted from manufacturing to capital management since the early 1970s, the cultural superstructure has also been remade, with no place for the image of labor. The paradigmatic artwork of this process would then quite possibly be Iselin Lønn's *Manpower Document* (1998–2001), an extraordinary bureaucratic prose poem or illustrated experimental novel that documents sixty days spent as an unskilled temporary worker in offices and canteens around Oslo.

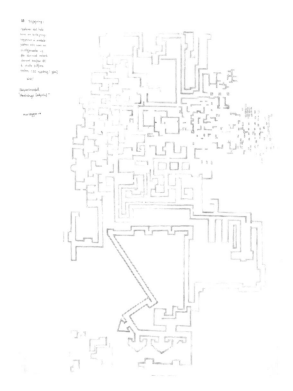

Iselin Lønn, *The Manpower Document* (1998–2001).
Courtesy of the artist.

If the central figure of Munch's *Workers in the Snow* was depicted
as possessing both individual agency and class consciousness,
Lønn's work is its future negative imprint. A narration of
the struggle to preserve an individual identity and coherent
subjectivity in the face of the raw, reductive relationship of wage
labor, the *Manpower Document* describes an atomizing process
that asks nothing of the worker but the bare minimum that any
interchangeable body could perform, that which allows no social
bonds to form and offers no access to solidarity, or even simple
friendship. Disorientated and depersonalized, Lønn responds
with calculated dissociation, taking the role of secret observer
and making meticulous maps of her workplaces. But even this
strategy of control unravels and the maps become surreal,
sprawling labyrinths, endlessly multiplying cubicles, and
corridors without exit.

In the new Oslo, of course, there is no space for such reflection: it comes pre-furnished with art; it overflows with art. The new Astrup Fearnley Museum, designed by Renzo Piano, with Franz West sculptures on the promenade. The Thief Hotel, designed by Ajas Mellbye, with Warhol in the lobby. The Norwegian Opera, designed by Snøhetta and decorated by Olafur Eliasson. Giant works by Pippilotti Rist and Eliasson, again, at the new Statoil headquarters. The promise of a new National Museum of Art, and still even the possibility of a new Munch Museum.

In order to discern the image of labor represented in these more recent developments, it is perhaps necessary to set aside the cultural analysis and resort to a more fundamental approach. In *Capital*, Karl Marx described the material results of the production process as representing labor-time crystallized into physical form. It is an image that seems strangely appropriate to the architecture of the new Fjord City and its satellites, with its repeated emphasis on crystalline forms. Here, it is not simply the labor of building that is on display, but the global labor force commanded by Norwegian-controlled capital, the surplus value extracted in China, Nigeria, and Brazil. Even Munch's painting of the workers in the snow, that had all of its confrontational power in 1910, has found a role as a masterpiece in the narrative that aims to normalize this extraordinary transfer of wealth, a narrative of entitlement to power that has crystallized into the icebergs and ziggurats of the new Oslo.

RISE UP WOMEN

Michala Paludan

OCCUPATIONAL REALISM

Julia Bryan-Wilson

1. Occupy: to hold a position or an office

In 1998, California-based artist Ben Kinmont began his longest and
most involved conceptual project to date: he opened his own bookselling business. The piece, which is ongoing, is entitled *Sometimes a nicer sculpture is being able to provide a living for your
family,* and Kinmont's use of the word "sculpture" harks back to
Joseph Beuys's notion of "social sculpture" as "how we shape our
thoughts into words [... and] how we mold and shape the world we
live in" (1993:19). Kinmont specializes in antiquarian books with a
focus on gastronomy, and in this capacity attends auctions, participates in bookfairs, works with libraries in need of development,
logs his inventory, negotiates prices, and ships books to private
and public collections around the world. *Sometimes a nicer sculpture* is meant to function both as an income-generating bookselling
trade and a performance that is legible as such in the art world.

For Kinmont, it is important that his business function *as a
business*; it is not enough for him to gesture symbolically towards
the world of commerce by, say, printing up ironic letterhead or
opening a fake storefront. As a result, he partakes in what I have
termed "occupational realism," in which the realm of waged labor
(undertaken to sustain oneself economically) and the realm of art
(pursued, presumably, for reasons that might include financial
gain, but that also exceed financialization and have aesthetic,
personal, and/or political motivations) collapse, becoming
indistinct or intentionally inverted. These are performances in

which artists enact the normal, obligatory tasks of work under the highly elastic rubric of "art." Here, the job becomes the art and the art becomes the job.

"Performance as occupation" participates in the rising tide of discourse regarding the interconnection of contingent labor, artistic value, and precarity. Precarity is one name given to the effect of neoliberal economic conditions emergent in the wake of global financial upheaval, recession, and the reorganization of employment to accommodate the spread of service, information, and knowledge work. It designates a pervasively unpredictable terrain of employment within these conditions—work that is without health care benefits or other safety nets, underpaid, part-time, unprotected, short-term, unsustainable, risky.[1] Debates about precarity—and an insistence that artists belong to the newly emerging "precariat"—have been increasingly taken up within contemporary art, as evidenced by exhibitions such as *The Workers: Precarity/Invisibility/Mobility,* which opened in 2011 at the Massachusetts Museum of Contemporary Art, as well as anthologies like *Critique of Creativity: Precarity, Subjectivity, and Resistance in the "Creative Industries"* (Raunig et al. 2011) and *Are You Working Too Much? Post-Fordism, Precarity, and the Labor of Art* (Aranda et al. 2011).[2] A group of cultural and educational laborers in London organized themselves into the Precarious Workers Brigade, and they have mobilized to protest arts funding cuts in the UK, the economic and power dynamics of unpaid internships, and other issues; their posters ask questions such as "Do you freelance but don't feel free?"

The ascendance of the term "precarity" connects to research in the last few years by sociologists such as Pascal Gielen, with his consideration of the congruence between artistic practices and post-Fordist economies (Gielen 2010). But this alleged congruence has wider consequences, as it underscores the need to understand artistic occupations temporally. As Pierre-Michel Menger's 2006 report on artistic employment notes, "the gap is widening" between brief vocations and lifelong careers:

How do short-term assignments translate into worker flows and careers? From a *labor supply* standpoint, one artist equals one long-term occupational prospect, especially when employment relationships are long-term and careers are well patterned. But the gap is widening between the vocational commitment and the way it transforms into a career: self-employment, freelancing and contingent work bring in discontinuity, repeated alternation between work, compensated and non-compensated unemployment, searching and networking activities, and cycling between multiple jobs inside or outside the arts.

(Menger 2006:4)

As Menger's text implies, the temporal mentality of artistic labor (contingent, intermittent, brief) has long resembled what is now called precarity. What happens, however, when artists—who, being popularly imagined as models of precarity *avant la lettre* as they do not earn steady wages in any conventional sense and have neither a secure employer nor a consistent, stable workplace— redefine art as work out of necessity, motored by a new urgency to "provide a living for your family," to cite Kinmont?

When I first conceived this essay, I wanted to provisionally define occupational realism as it functions both as a genre or style of performance as well as an attitude towards work that sheds light on the specific class conditions of artistic production and identity. Within economics, to think occupationally means to think variously about professional status or employment; feminism further understands nonremunerative labors such as housework or childcare, traditionally performed by women, as occupations. As I have been writing, and as the Occupy movement has grown around the world, I have been further impelled to rethink how "occupation" in terms of a spatial political strategy might connect to "occupational" practices that specifically interrogate labor and value. If occupational realism stems at least partially from jobs or work undertaken by artists because they "have to" (though the issue of compulsion, need, and choice is unevenly applicable), this form of practice also raises questions about the potential strategic or operational value of precarity: its capacity to redefine social relations, aesthetic and affective production, and class structures.

In addition, the language used to describe the current conditions of precarity draws heavily upon the rhetoric of performance, as performance skates the line between live art and art that is lived. According to theorist Paolo Virno, post-Fordist capitalism, with its emphasis on flexibility, has led to an expansion of "living labor," such that not only all of our working hours, but our very desires and thoughts have been absorbed into new regimes of work (2004:53). But Virno sees a space of political possibility within what he calls "virtuosity," which "happens to the artist or performer who, after performing, does not leave a work of art behind" (in Gielen and Lavaert 2009).[3] Within his formulation, artistic performance (which in some Marxist understandings is posited as the paradigmatic outside, alternative, or other to deadening alienated wage labor) as a form of activity that generates surplus value without an end product, has become not a specialized case unique to performers, dancers, musicians, and the like, but has turned into the general condition of "servile" waged work. Virno writes: "The affinity between a pianist and a waiter, which Marx had foreseen, finds an unexpected confirmation in the epoch in which all wage labor has something in common with the 'performing artist'" (2004:68).

Virno sees virtuosity as a way to move beyond narrow considerations of political action, artistic production, and work as existing in separate spheres. For Virno, the virtuoso's activity "finds its own fulfillment" and must include an audience or "witnesses"; he stipulates that it contain some sort of public or social component (52). Virno relies heavily upon the language of theatre; he discusses the performance, the script, the score, and the audience as he charts an opening out from work to the realms of cultural or creative activity, and finally into the sphere of the political (56). But what about artists who move in the other direction and mine the procedures of labor in the service of their performances? How does occupational realism thematize and make legible the conditions that Virno describes, as well as indicate what Virno overlooks?

2. Occupy: to fill up (time or space)

Kinmont's assertion that his business is his art is hardly exceptional. In one sense, such an assertion is a conceptual art strategy that began in the early 20th century with Marcel Duchamp, in which something (either an object or an idea or a gesture) is appropriated, put into quotes, framed, nominated, or bracketed "as art." In the wake of this logic, art's very contours loosened and blurred to accommodate two of its ostensible opposites: "life" and "work." There is, however, a key distinction between post-Duchampian strategies of nomination and artists who begin to understand that if their activities already resemble art, they might as well name them as such. Here, they do not "decide" to feel or think of their life or work as art, but just the opposite: they start feeling and thinking it before they know it, because of the effects that Virno describes.

Indeed, the art-into-life experiments of the early 1960s—in which virtually any thing or activity could be redefined as art (such as Alison Knowles's *Make a Salad,* 1962)—led to a flowering of late-20th-century artists declaring their jobs to be art.[4] In 1966 Canadian artist duo Iain and Ingrid Baxter formed N.E. Thing Co. Ltd. (they legally incorporated in 1969), and until 1978 mimed the procedures of business, including printing up business cards, attending conventions, and even sponsoring a junior hockey team. Though the Baxters aimed to be a moneymaking enterprise, their satirical take on the trappings of corporate culture and bureaucracy "did not yield the sustainable economic base, which they envisioned" (Lauder 2010:57–58). Similarly, Gordon Matta-Clark and Carol Goodden's New York City art project/ functioning restaurant *Food,* opened in 1971, was shuttered after two years because they could not make it a viable business.

While some artists have pursued a corporate model, others have individually taken on temporary working-class identities. To list only a few: in Linda Mary Montano's *Odd Jobs,* 1973, the artist announced her availability to do housework such as light hauling, cleaning cellars, interior painting, or gardening. She did so in part to transform, mentally and affectively, the labor she was already doing to make money. As she wrote, "I liked what I was doing when I called it art" (Montano 1981:n.p.). After finding a nurse's dress in a thrift store, Montano offered herself up for house calls to sick friends and printed cards that listed her skills and services, including "massage, chicken soup, visits, temperature taking, and forehead holding, etc." The nurse outfit not only functioned as an apparently visible confirmation of her abilities to perform these tasks, it also lent some credibility to her capacities by acting as an authorizing uniform. Montano's piece resonates with recent writings by Italian feminist Silvia Federici, who has discussed how debates on precarity have under-theorized the role of women's reproductive and household labor (2008). Such feminist perspectives are vital, especially since one substantial vein of occupational realism involves women artists such as Marina Abramović, Cosey Fanni Tutti, and Nikki S. Lee "performing" sex work to explore questions of sexualized service (see Bryan-Wilson 2012).

Other examples: Bonnie Sherk flipped hamburger patties during the graveyard shift on weekend stints under the title *Short Order Cook,* 1974, at a San Francisco, California, diner called *Andy's Donuts* as part of her extended exploration into gender, labor, and what she referred to as "cultural costumes" (in Bradley 2005:189). In a snapshot documentation of this piece, Sherk is caught in action by the griddle with her floppy white chef's hat. She also redefined a job she had as a waitress as a performance, entitling it *Waitress;* in such pieces, her customers were by and large not aware that as she was serving food, she was also playing a role as a self-conscious artistic act. The work was made available as a performance to an art audience primarily when photographs such as these circulated in art contexts.

In 1981, artist Tony Labat trained to be a professional boxer in *Fight: A Practical Romance*—a pugilistic piece that, when seen alongside Montano's domestic housework, raises questions about the performance and exaggeration of gender difference. More recently, in 2000 Bulgarian-born Daniel Bozhkov undertook a performance in which he worked at a Maine Wal-Mart as a "people greeter." This piece, entitled *Training in Assertive Hospitality,* involved him helping customers navigate the store; between shifts, he also painted a fresco in the Layaway Department. A photo of the artist in uniform shows Bozhkov in one of the aisles of the store, an American flag hanging behind him; his Wal-Mart issued vest is laden with text indicating that he is there to serve, including the question "How may I help YOU?" Bozhkov's piece demonstrates that occupational realists put their emphasis on mainstream employment structures; such artists might experience, as a side benefit, coming into contact with different communities, but stand at some remove from social art practices in which those interactions are the central focus. Though relational projects also contest the boundaries between art and work, artists whose works com prises organic farming, community outreach, or public-policy advocacy use their practice as a way to engage with, produce, and actively envision *alternative* economies, rather than directly inserting themselves into *normative* economies, as occupational realists do.

The roster of artists who embody the joint roles of performer/worker does not include the many artists who investigate the realm of wage labor by employing workers in the space of the art institution, such as Oscar Bony. For his project *Familia Obrera,* 1968 (Working Class Family), Bony paid a blue-collar worker, machinist Luis Ricardo Rodríguez, along with his wife and their 10-year-old son, twice Rodríguez's normal hourly wage to sit on a pedestal during an art exhibition at the Instituto Di Tella in Buenos Aires (Cullen 2008:90). By contrast, occupational realists insist on *doing the work themselves,* standing bodily in the space of labor. Hence they are also distinct from artists like Santiago Sierra, whose performances involve hiring workers to carry out menial tasks, sometimes within the space of the art institution. Sierra presents workers as objects to be watched, and this spectacularization frequently removes workers from their usual labor (at least for the duration of the art event). By contrast, occupational realists like Kinmont, Sherk, or Bozhkov do art as they work, within the normal contexts and spaces of work, and they work as they do art; this precise overlap, simultaneity, and multiplicity is crucial.

If most occupational realists are uninterested in putting their labor within the context of traditional museum or gallery display, they are equally uninterested in what could be called theatricality, if we use the basic definition of theatricality to mean "of or for the stage." Other meanings of theatricality—that which is marked by pretense, extravagant exhibitionism, or artificial emotion—further highlight what these artists are intentionally *not* doing. In fact, they often do not want their customers or colleagues to witness or acknowledge what they do as art—they want to vocationally "pass." Kinmont speculates that few of his customers are aware that his bookselling is also an art project—and if they are aware, they are prone to take him less seriously as a dealer. That is, though Virno's idea of the virtuoso demands an audience, that audience is here complicated and fractured—there is a "work" audience which need not or should not know that one of its workers has a value-added position as an artist, and then there is the "art" audience.

Oakland-based artist Sean Fletcher commenced *Becoming a Life Insurance Salesman as a Work of Art* (1996–2002) after he realized he could not survive on his art practice alone and had to take a salaried job. As a relic from his performance illustrates, he signed, dated, and numbered the back of some of his business cards, remaking them into a "limited edition" artwork. Fletcher was fired when his bosses discovered that he was curating small shows in his office after hours, thus violating some of the protocol of the business world by taking up space during non-work hours, and inviting people into the office who had "no business" being there. These performances tell us something about the temporality of precarity: unlike a weekend inhabitation, or a permanent condition, jobs exist for unpredictable time spans before people rotate away, move on, are laid off, quit. Occupational realism as a performance mode unfolds in similarly vague registers of time—a few years here, a few years there, so that its durational aspect hovers between the brief or temporary and the lifelong. Fletcher's project demonstrates that both the art performance and life insurance position demand that he present *himself* as a coherent product to be trusted and valued. As "self-branding" has become a prevalent ideology of contemporary life, artists who make themselves and their business into their art unmask how the emphasis on self-marketing and entrepreneurialism long known to artists now pressures many neoliberal subjects.

Some occupational realism echoes classic ethnographic or investigative reporting techniques in which scholars or reporters become embedded among their observational subjects. In fact, Barbara Ehrenreich's bestselling book from 2001, *Nickel and Dimed: On (Not) Getting By in America,* in which she spent three months doing unskilled labor in order to determine conditions of living on a low wage, took up precisely the same sorts of jobs as some of the artists just mentioned (food service like Sherk, cleaning houses like Montano, working at Wal-Mart like Bozhkov). As Ehrenreich discovered, the idea that she was "deceiving" anyone quickly unraveled: "There's no way, for example, to pretend to be a waitress: the food either gets to the table or it doesn't. People knew me as a waitress, a cleaning person, a nursing home aide, or a retail clerk not because I acted like one, but because that's what I *was,* at least for the time I was with them" (2001:9). Yes and no: Ehrenreich assumes intimate knowledge about low-wage life in a very brief amount of time but never turned to these jobs, as many do, out of true desperation. She follows the long tradition of journalistic *exposés* about the deprivations of working-class life (think of Nellie Bly going undercover in a Pittsburgh factory in the late 19th century).

Ehrenreich insists that she is not a "blue collar wannabe" but establishes rules of approach, somewhat like a sociologist, before plunging in to "get her hands dirty" (4). Ehrenreich was castigated by some critics for the overlay of elitism and arrogance in her project. This is one major bone of contention with occupational realism, too, in its least nuanced iterations: it taps into longstanding downwardly mobile pretensions among educated, leftist artists and writers alike, pretensions that veer close to class condescension. As one review of *Nickel and Dimed* stated:

> The presumptions within cross-class narratives need to be made similarly apparent: that only someone outside of the experience of economic subjection can accurately document the physical and psychological trauma of that process; that only someone with economic privilege can call upon the sociological methodology necessary to name economic pain.
>
> (Schocket 2003:49)

However, some artists who take on the role of low-wage worker as art, like Montano, are less interested in narrating economic pain than in transforming a range of "experiences"—always admittedly limited or partial—in art. This is a persistent claim of self-aware class difference: *I know that what I'm doing right now is just a job, a job that occupies some of my time, but I have some other identity that validates me.* Educated artists might choose to be blue-collar workers with little training, but that directional flow is usually one way, for when untrained workers decide to be artists, they are often considered "outsiders"—like janitor Henry Darger, whose work is labeled as "outsider art" to mark his distance from the usual classed routes of artistic training.

The privileges of re-employment are reserved for elite mobility, in which, for example, a Wall Street broker decides to reskill as a baker, a downwardly mobile shift that is belied by the cultural capital it trades in and is correspondingly narrated as laden with intangible psychic rewards, the rewards of doing "personally gratifying" labor. One such narrative, in which a University of Chicago PhD became a mechanic and extolled the virtues of his newfound honest labor, was told by Matthew Crawford in his (like Ehrenreich's, bestselling) book *Shop Class as Soulcraft: An Inquiry into the Value of Work* (2009). Others further down the class ladder, however, may not have such choices available to them—a laidoff mechanic cannot move easily into more upwardly mobile realms of employment. Contingency—which was lauded in the 1990s as a potentially radical or productive mode of thinking about art and identity formation—has curdled into the grim uncertainties of precarity.

The class-based friction felt by Ehrenreich's critics does not accompany every project of occupational realism, especially those in which an artist becomes a knowledge worker or businessman. In Kinmont's *Sometimes a nicer sculpture,* for instance, the class shift from artist-as-information-peddler to specialized bookseller does not seem so dramatic, or so fantastical. Kinmont absorbs into his business his interest in archives and the production of knowledge, and then rotates his bookselling knowledge back into art again, a cycle tinged with the masculine imperative to be the family breadwinner.

When the distinctions between art and work are eroded, does the capacity for art to critique the regimes of work likewise evaporate? Such an erasure might seem, rather, to serve neoliberal paradigms, in which all hours of the day are subsumed under the rubric of productivity. As Virno notes, the distinction between being at work and being off work (at home in domestic space or elsewhere in leisure time), has shifted into the more arbitrary differences between "remunerated life and non-remuner-ated life" (2004:103). (As any freelancer knows, if you are never officially on the clock, then you never feel totally off the clock, either.)

It has been argued that, within the dotcom boom of the late 1990s, artistic work with its variable hours and its adaptable working conditions became a model for "creative" informational work like software development, and thus the critical or even antagonistic aspects of art were subsumed into byproducts of what Richard Florida trumpeted as the lifestyle-as-product of the "creative class" (2002). The optimistically heralded professionalization of art—as in Daniel Pink's proclamation that the Master of Fine Arts degree "is the new MBA"—signaled not only that (some) artists stood to make a lot of money doing design or content work, but that professionals were being redefined as artists (2005:54). And what is for sale or highly valued in this new professional creative class is something akin to professional style. At the cusp of the post-industrial turn, C. Wright Mills noted that what is on offer with the professionalization of work has become a matter of attitude and affect—what he calls marketable personality (1951:241).

Importantly, "occupational realism" as a phrase has other meanings that resonate beyond the art world, notably emerging in education, behavioral psychology, and sociology in the mid-1950s to discuss the structuration of class mobility and the relative lack of ease of moving from one class position to another in the United States. This research, proliferating within academic departments of social work, education, and counseling for the last few decades, discusses the discrepancy between levels of aspiration in adolescents or first-time job seekers and their "actual" potential to achieve those aspirations (see Coffee 1957; Stokes 1977; Paap 1997). Within this context, occupational realism means, to put it simplistically, how much someone's planned-for job matches his/her eventual employment, how realistic one is about one's eventual occupation. To desire to be a plumber when one "grows up," and to be enrolled in a vocational program in which one would acquire plumbing skills is to have a firm sense of occupational realism.

To desire to be a world-famous astronaut when one is an economically disadvantaged student with bad grades and test scores (which themselves gauge and measure class status) is to express a low degree of occupational realism. In other words, how closely do your fantasies hew to your already-determined class station, to your access to cultural capital, to the role you are expected to play? According to these studies, for certain subjects (especially those that are low income, nonwhite, and/or female), if those fantasies are mismatched, quality of life plummets when they enter the workforce (Thomas 1976). To imagine a life other than the one you were handed is, in these studies, to set yourself up for failure; it is better to aspire down than to aspire up.

Taking into account the strictures on class mobility, these studies emphasize that within the US, movement out of one class and into another is infrequent and exceptional. They also emphasize that the adult's question to the child, "What do you want to be?" is not only fundamentally about identity (the molding of selfhood into the shapes disciplined by work) but also about forecasting and projecting into the future—a future that is marked by labor structuration along lines of class, race, and gender, and increasingly considered precarious. One influential study from 1966, based on a national survey of children and teenagers in the US, *The Adolescent Experience,* found strong gender-based differences between the boys and girls they studied in terms of wishes for their future selves: "Girls do not show the same level of clear and active realism in regards to mobility. The girl's future must in some sense remain ambiguous—it depends so much on sexual realization and being chosen in marriage" (Douvan and Adelson 1966:78). This striking passage brings up complex, and painful, questions of volition and agency, not least as it relates to gender. We must account for the discrepant meanings of "occupational realism" here: for artists, it is about an educated choice to redefine remunerated labor within the value structure of art. The educational/vocational usage of "occupational realism," which describes the necessity of being *realistic about class limitations,* demonstrates that "job choice" is for some only illusory, and for others an obvious mark of privilege.

3. Occupy: to seize possession of and maintain control over

In 2005, South Korean–born artist Bohyun Yoon circulated a
postcard on which he declared his upcoming performance piece,
Two Year Soldier Project. As he explains, "As a male Korean
citizen, I have to serve in the military for two years. At the time, I
thought of myself as an artist, so I 'disguised' myself as a soldier
for two years" (Yoon 2011a). Compulsory military service, national
obligation, and creative authorial intent collide as the artist
declares himself to be "undercover," a double agent in his own
mind. Within this piece, he might appear to all observers to be
embodying the position of soldier, but his self-identification as an
artist—one who was physically and logistically unable to make
material objects for a designated amount of time—also distinctly
imbues his military actions with extra value because he executes
them as an artistic performance.

That he embodies this work of soldiering differently (at a critical
remove, perhaps, or conversely, with fiercer concentration?) is
somewhat implied, yet we would have no sense of this difference
if it were not for the postcard announcement's photograph of him
wearing a handmade transparent vinyl camouflage outfit, a glass
helmet, and holding a blown-glass gun, an outfit that he obviously did not don when actually on duty. "No opening reception,
not open to the public" states the text on the back of the postcard.
The formal declaration of this artistic "disguise" presumably fell
away once he enlisted and, sans glass accessories, was indistinguishable from the others with whom he trained and worked.

The bohemian *déclassé* drag of some artists (such as Sherk) as
they dipped in and out of the working-class labor force is distinct
from the literal demands made upon Yoon. His status change was
beyond his control: his decision to reinvent his military service
as part and parcel of his art was in response to his lack of choice.
Yoon has an MFA and was trained in the glass department of the
Rhode Island School of Design; he wanted to stay in the United
States after he graduated but in order to extend his visa, he had

to return to South Korea and carry out his conscripted military service. On his postcard (which was circulated to a US audience in advance of his enlistment), Yoon shows himself at-the-ready, facing the viewer with his gun in hand, a parodic stance made absurd by his transparent outfit that produces the opposite effect intended by camouflage, as it renders him more visible, more vulnerable, more open, and more at risk. His hand-blown glass gun and glass helmet, in addition to being nonfunctional, are likewise fragile and might shatter with impact.

The glass helmet is the only material artifact from Yoon's two-year piece, aside from the postcard, journal entries, and the two-year gap from 2005 to 2007 evident on his CV, which otherwise shows a busy itinerary of group and solo exhibitions. During this period he was engaged in his all-consuming performance without access to his own art-making tools or materials. Interestingly, however, during his active service in the military, Yoon primarily worked as a graphic designer—the same sort of job he might have had if he was supporting himself as an artist invested in material forms of art making. At the same time, this graphic design work was done under the scrutiny of the military with the constraints of their harsh schedule, and he endured a significant amount of militaristic mental training.

Yoon's two-year piece also summons the idea of occupation as militaristically conquered space—though for him, the space of occupation was not land, but his own head. He is now working to minimize or work through the experience, to expel from his mind the procedures of the training. He has described himself while in the military as both occupied and preoccupied: distracted by his soldiering from his normal thoughts. It is a preoccupation that now requires undoing; since he left the military, Yoon has focused his art on interrogating systems of social control.

As a performance, *Two Year Soldier Piece* asks: What is the work here, where is it manifested, how does it become legible, and what are the mechanisms of its materialization? *Two Year Soldier*

Project (whose after-effects continue to resonate through Yoon's art and thinking) insists upon the non-identity between the worker and the job, opening up a space between being and doing. In the above discussion, I mentioned vocational "passing," but perhaps that is not the right phrase with regards to occupational realism. For the idea of passing presumes one stable identity, permanency, or authenticity against which drag is thrown into relief. What Yoon's performance makes clear or renders transparent is that, under precarious conditions, one switches between radically different positions and/or occupations, performing differently according to shifting circumstances.

Still, I use the contested word *realism* to signal that performances of this sort are not just "acts" (though they are suffused with potential irony). At the same time, neither are they about unmediated access to anything that might be called "real"—itself always fugitive, phantasmatic, and illusory. Within theatre history, realism signifies a range of practices that began in the 19th century in opposition to the romantic dramas popular at the time, including naturalism, which often depicted bodies at work and/or at leisure in extended mediations upon the two (see Styan 1981). Within art history, Realism refers to a school of painting that originated in France in the 19th century. It was championed by Gustave Courbet and was understood as a politicized reaction to the 1848 Revolution, in which artists felt they were charged with showing the structures of social and political relations with all their ambiguities, including "class conflict and expropriation" (Clark 1973:116). Courbet was not the first artist to depict labor or laboring bodies— but he meaningfully placed peasant labor next to his own labor as an artist, thereby producing resonate homologies. Occupational realism, which began in the late 1960s and early 1970s along with postindustrial economic changes, likewise reveals ambiguous, difficult, and unresolvable conflicts about class, including professionalization, waged work, and volition.

Beyond theatre or art historical notions of Realism as a critical style, these artists are "realists" in the sense that they are insistent about the overlap between realms of art and work. Artists like Kinmont or Yoon or Fletcher effectively function as booksellers or soldiers or life insurance salesmen. They perform their duties within the actual sites of bookselling and soldiering and salesmanship. In addition, they are employed within the discourses of state-enforced, economically prescribed self-identifications, in which everything from census forms to visa applications ask us to name our occupation (meaning business, or legitimate wage work) with a singular word or phrase. What position do you fill? What space do you regularly occupy? These artists undermine the singular grammar demanded by these questions, as they perform roles as both artists and as wage earners. For artists whose employment becomes their art, their lives are dually occupied, toggling across the slash: bookseller/artist, artist/ military man. Yet for Yoon, who did not have the privileges associated with educated white males with US citizenship in a time without a military draft, the question of "choice" proves much more volatile.

4. Occupy: to engage or employ the attention of

Within capitalism, art has long figured as a special type of production. It is also understood to catalyze a special type of sensory orientation; doing something "as art" is meant to increase attention or awareness on the part of the doer. In Montano's *Odd Jobs,* she took on work not only as a way to generate money but also to shift her own affective stance towards activities which otherwise seemed onerous, boring, or laborious. In a related vein, Mierle Laderman Ukeles in 1976 asked 300 maintenance workers in a building in New York to reconsider their work as art for one hour a day, in her piece *I Make Maintenance Art One Hour Every Day.*[5] She gave out buttons emblazoned with the title for the participants to wear and documented workers as they went about their business in an effort to destabilize the distinctions between dignified art-making and presumably rote, even numbing tasks such as sweeping or vacuuming. Ukeles did not dictate how her newly nominated artists would go about their "maintenance art," and there was a range of responses (from amusement to suspicion that she was working for the US Department of Immigration). In the end, the piece attempted to unsettle ideas that art exists in a sphere separate from non-commodity-producing service work.

What does it mean to be at work but not occupied—that is, not fully devoting one's attentions to the task at hand? Is this partial focus assumed to be the condition of most contemporary work? How might art also speak to this space of mental elsewhereness? The idea that "art is a calling," demanding full presence, increasingly does not hold up, as plenty of art is outsourced to others, is made during states of boredom, or even explicitly thematizes distraction, and much "work" is performed with vigilant, intense, or reverent focus. In the past few years, when I have mentioned the likes of Ukeles, Yoon, or Fletcher in my classes, my students want to know how these differently interpellated workers *felt* about what they were doing, as if in response to some pervasive desire for art to be personally transformative. Did the attitudes of the maintenance crew change in the wake of Ukeles's intervention? Did Yoon or Fletcher have a different mental or emotional relationship to training for war or selling insurance because they had been designated "performances"?

My students have been frustrated by their lack of access to the thought-processes involved, especially irritated at how Yoon and Fletcher have corrupted what is romanticized as an activity apart from the sphere of work—art—and turned it into a form of toil that seems to offer no emotive surplus, no aesthetic dimension, no moral lesson. This frustration points to the stubborn residue that clings to authorially invested artistic activity; the intent of the artist still carries disproportional significance. When precarious work—flexible, contingent, parttime—closely resembles artistic labor, at least outwardly, does the main distinction between art and work remain an internal thought process, a feeling, an attitude? How "committed" are these artists to inhabiting their roles, how much control or manipulation of their emotional life do they exercise? Their performances succeed, in part, to the degree that they disappear, at least to us witnesses, into the contours of their labor. There is no way to measure how the free-floating frame of "performance" might have an impact on the "work" these artists did: they had no script to follow, no character to play, no narrative to trace.

But the ultimately unknowable interiorities of Ukeles, Yoon, and Fletcher are of less concern than the question of uncertain valuation. These performances insist that there might be some separation of intent from activity, some division of labor in which the activity's registration as art remains distinct from that of work—that is, in the realm of affect. What is more, the actions of these artists are granted an extra sheen of value; the added component of artistic labor, however immaterial, implies that the self-reflexive performer might have a different level of awareness about their work than does the ordinary worker. For his part, Fletcher always considered himself fully both an artist and a salesman. He did his job during the day, but was also preoccupied with his after-hours art career. For Yoon, during his two years, even when in uniform, his answer to the question "What do you do?" varied depending on who was asking (Yoon 2011b). These definitions and identifications are messy, partial, and contingent.

Hito Steyerl's recent take on art and labor places occupations in opposition to waged work: "An occupation keeps people busy instead of giving them paid labor" (Steyerl 2011). But for some artists, occupations are routes into artistic value and meaning, as well as to remuneration. I asked Kinmont if he feels differently doing his bookselling job knowing that it is art. He is a perfect case study since he had worked as a bookseller previous to *Sometimes a nicer sculpture,* but in that previous employment he had not considered the work an art piece. He responded:

> I think I do, absolutely, think about it differently. It has
> to do with how you chose to define art. For me, art is about

an awareness of the creation of meaning. Deciding that
it is art is a tool or a device by which to see how it is
meaningful to me. It helps me align my priorities. Sometimes
it is still drudgery or tedious—the backbreaking, dirty, boring
work of packing up books—but it is also meaningful to me
to work in the area of cultural preservation and to contribute
to my family.

(Kinmont 2011)

Crucial here, again, is the fact that attentiveness trumps
Duchampian nomination; this is not a one-time act, but an
ongoing process of consideration paid to conditions that already
exist. Kinmont has described this as a relatively taxing method
of working, akin to bilingualism, since the languages and codes
of one value structure are so different from the other and he finds
himself constantly translating from one to another.

5. Occupy: to seize possession of and maintain control over

"THIS IS MY OCCUPATION," reads a sign held aloft at an Occupy
Wall Street demonstration in fall 2011—bringing together in one
terse phrase multiple definitions of employment, work, claiming
territory, political strategy, and affective absorption. In 1953, art
critic Clement Greenberg wrote an essay in which he considered
the crisis of culture and speculated about its future, given the rapid
economic changes around him in the postwar context:

> The only solution that I can conceive of under these
> conditions is to shift its center of gravity away from leisure
> and place it squarely in the middle of work. Am I suggesting
> something whose outcome could no longer be called culture,
> since it would not depend on leisure? I am suggesting
> something whose outcome I cannot imagine.
>
> (1961:32)

Greenberg's prophecy rings true as the unimaginable relocation of culture to work continues to unfold in the 21st century. Certainly what I am calling occupational realism will shift in relation to this new focus on occupation and intention—as with Greenberg, I find myself at a loss to imagine what exactly that might look like. But let me conclude by offering some thoughts based on my historical understanding of a time when art also went to work.

If we are witnessing a whole-scale economic shift whose only known contour is its very unmappability, its instability and uncertainty, in which workers of all kinds, diverse in their class status and in their various degrees of cultural capital, survive on the barest of margins, with no sense of security or futurity, then it could be that artists engaged in occupational realism prefigured the collapsing categories of work, performance, and art in precarious times. The Occupy movement has spawned several artists' groups interested in foregrounding their own underpaid and undervalued labor as art workers, including an Arts and Labor contingent of Occupy Wall Street and an artists' bloc at Occupy San Francisco. Many in these groups are reclaiming the phrase "art worker"—a term that has been deployed at various moments in the history of the avantgarde, beginning with Russian construc-tivism, the 1930s Artists' Union that emerged when artists were employed through the US Works Progress Administration, and the Art Workers' Coalition, founded in 1969 in New York City. Those affiliated with the AWC called themselves "art workers," a term I used for the title of my 2009 book *Art Workers: Radical Practice in the Vietnam War Era* as a historical nod to these artists' own self-descriptors. By no means did I take it as an untroubled term. It had uneven currency within its own moment, as my book elaborates, and was fraught with ambivalence, failure, and contradiction (Bryan-Wilson 2009).

So I am curious, if not vaguely mystified, by how the category of the "art worker" is being resurrected. Does its most recent resurfacing mean that artists are interested in reclaiming the phrase with all of its blind spots and fault lines? What the Occupy movement's canny focus on the "99%" has offered us is a way of finding alliances without recourse to categories such as "the working class." The Occupy movement has made clear that "workers" are no longer a coherent category, and hence to organize around any single notion of employment, given its instabilities and multiplicities, makes little sense. A slogan that declares "artists are the 99%" speaks to the economic conditions of most artists, who often piece together part-time work to pay the rent, teach in adjunct positions, have mountains of student debt from their art degree, and lack health insurance.

But I want to think hard about what the phrase "art worker" means, its inconsistencies and its elisions. Is the reemergence of the term "art worker" a recognition of the pervasive blurring of art into labor, or is it an overly simplistic conflation of *artist* and *worker,* yoking those two together unproblematically? If we can admit there is no such thing as one kind of "worker," then we need to account for the fact that who we call "artists" are likewise not a coherent category. We must keep in our focus the global art industry that maintains its connections to and is integrally part of the 1%. We need to parse distinctions that threaten to collapse: not all art is work, not all work is art, and the class distinctions embedded within these terms still matter. Cultural production is a specialized, or as Hans Abbing calls it, "exceptional" form of work, one that has ties to markets, alternative or gift economies, and affective labor (Abbing 2002).[6] We should not erase distinctions or lose a sense of nuance in order to call for solidarity. Instead, we should theorize the complexities of art that span dematerialized performance as well as object-making.

As an anonymous open letter to the Art Workers' Coalition in 1969 phrased it:

> The word "workers" in the name [of the AWC] is a hopeful sign [...]. Suppose however that the AWC were to declare something like "all power to the workers." In saying this they would not need to be repeating the old slogans of art

in the service of the revolution which seems to have produced neither good art nor any revolution at all. Rather they might be saying that art belongs to all who can grasp it and draw energy from it. What this means in practical terms I don't know ... The cry "all power to the workers" means just that, "all power to *all* workers." It does not mean that the oyster dredgers control blue points and the artists control acrylics. It means that energy glows as evenly as possible from each segment of society to all others; and when that happens the moral equivalent to privilege will have been found.

(Smithsonian Institute 1969)

Though this letter strikes a hopeful note, the AWC never managed to bridge its concerns with the inequalities outside of the art world. The Art Workers' Coalition, in its lifespan from 1969–71, did accomplish many things, including an incisive institutional critique that helped illuminate connections between artistic industries, the military, and corporations. They agitated for more oversight in the art world in a time, then as now, with vast inequalities and a star system that rewards some and not others. But the AWC should function less as a triumphant moment than as a cautionary tale: it fell apart in part because it did not offer a sustainable analysis of the co-articulation of race, class, and gender. The art workers circa 1970 were never fully able to recognize this key fact: artists often have, and use, many class-based privileges that many other workers do not have, not the least of which is access to cultural capital.

How have these precarious times changed how we conceive of both art and work? If we take our cue from Virno, we might speculate that our notion of performance has undergone vast transformations that bleed from the cultural to the economic. Yet the contingencies upon which the idea of "artist" or "performer" rests have always in part been based on class privilege, an aspect that is underexplored in Virno. I might go so far as to say that "art-ists" are not "workers," which is precisely what makes occupational realism legible as a form of practice—there is a gap between these nonidentical categories wide enough that their bridging feels surprising. If art were already work, or work were already art, these projects that redefine art as work and vice versa would simply fail to register as inversions, as conceptual frames, or as critiques. For many people, working and struggling to survive financially makes creating art less possible; at the same time, work contains within it the possibilities to envision new sorts of relations. As Kathi Weeks puts it, "Work is not only a site of exploitation, domination, and antagonism, but also where we might find the power to create alternatives on the basis of subordinated knowledges, resistant subjectivities, and emergent models of organization" (2011:29). Potentially, the freshly minted art workers of the Occupy movement will not fixate on getting a bigger piece of the artmarket pie, and instead will continue to instigate a robust, subtle, and complex analysis of economic conditions attuned to larger struggles against inequality. This is a moment to talk openly about privilege, debt, economic justice, and art as a space of imaginative possibility that has the potential to transform how we think about work, and performance.

Notes

[1] For more on risk as constitutive of the "new modernity," see Beck (1992).

[2] As this cluster of activity suggests, 2011 was an especially fertile year for conversations about precarity, the recession, and artistic production. See also "Precarity: The People's Tribunal," convened at London's Institute of Contemporary Arts in March 2011, and Hal Foster's article about Thomas Hirschhorn's "precarious practice" (2011:28–30).

[3] In her essay in this issue, Shannon Jackson usefully complicates Virno's definition of "virtuosity" through the lens of theatre, dance, and music as opposed to visual art (Jackson 2012).

[4] For an intelligent and comprehensive look at a wide range of artists (from Yves Klein to Kinmont) who explicitly engage with the commercial sphere, see Luis Jacob, *Commerce by Artists* (2011).

[5] For more on Ukeles, see Molesworth (2000) and Jackson (2011).

[6] Gregory Sholette (2011) has also written extensively on the "dark matter" and unacknowledged labor that motors the art industry.

References

Abbing, Hans. 2002. *Why Are Artists Poor? The Exceptional Economy of the Arts*. Amsterdam: Amsterdam University Press.

Aranda, Julieta, Brian Kuan Wood, and Anton Vidokle, eds. 2011. *Are You Working Too Much? Post-Fordism, Precarity, and the Labor of Art*. E-flux journal. Berlin: Sternberg Press.

Beck, Ulrich. 1992. *Risk Society: Towards a New Modernity*. Trans. Mark Ritter. London: Sage Publications.

Beuys, Joseph. 1993. *Joseph Beuys in America: Energy Plan for the Western Man. Writings by and Interviews with the Artist*. Ed. Carin Kuoni. New York: Four Walls Eight Windows.

Bradley, Will. 2005. "Let it Grow." *frieze* 94 (October):189.

Bryan-Wilson, Julia. 2009. *Art Workers: Radical Practice in the Vietnam War Era*. Berkeley: University of California Press.

———2012. "Dirty Commerce: Art Work and Sex Work since the 1970s." *differences: A Journal of Feminist Cultural Studies* 23, 2:71–112.

Clark, T.J. 1973. *Image of the People: Gustave Courbet and the 1848 Revolution*. London: Thames and Hudson.

Coffee, James Madison. 1957. "Occupational Realism: An Analysis of Factors Influencing Realism in the Occupational Planning of High School Seniors." PhD diss. Cambridge, MA: Harvard Graduate School of Education.

Crawford, Matthew. 2009. *Shop Class as Soulcraft: An Inquiry into the Value of Work*. New York: Penguin Press.

Cullen, Deborah. 2008. *Arte ≠ Vida: Actions by Artists of the Americas 1960–2000*. New York: El Museo del Barrio.

Douvan, Elizabeth, and Joseph Adelson. 1966. *The Adolescent Experience*. New York: Wiley.

Ehrenreich, Barbara. 2001. *Nickel and Dimed: On (Not) Getting By in America*. New York: Metropolitan Books.

Federici, Silvia. 2008. "Precarious Labor: A Feminist Viewpoint." *In the Middle of a Whirlwind (Whirlwinds),* 6 June. http://inthemiddleofthewhirlwind.wordpress. com/precarious-labor-a-feminist-viewpoint/ (3 July 2011).

Florida, Richard. 2002. *The Rise of the Creative Class: And How It's Transforming Work, Leisure, Community and Everyday Life.* New York: Basic Books.

Foster, Hal. 2011. "Crossing Over: The Precarious Practice of Thomas Hirschhorn." *The Berlin Journal* 20 (Spring):28–30.

Gielen, Pascal. 2010. *The Murmuring of the Artistic Multitude: Global Art, Memory and Post-Fordism.* Amsterdam: Valiz.

———, and Sonja Lavaert. 2009. "The Dismeasure of Art: An Interview with Paolo Virno." *Stichting Kunst en Openbare Ruimte, Open* 17. http://classic.skor.nl/article-4178-nl.html?lang=en (10 December 2011).

Greenberg, Clement. 1961. "The Plight of Culture." In *Art and Culture: Critical Essays,* 22–34. Boston, MA: Beacon Press.

Jackson, Shannon. 2011. *Social Works: Performing Art, Supporting Publics.* London: Routledge.

———. 2012. "Just-in-Time: Performance and the Aesthetics of Precarity." TDR 56, 4 (T216):10–31.

Jacob, Luis, ed. 2011. *Commerce by Artists.* Toronto: Art Metropole.

Kinmont, Ben. 2011. Phone interview with the author, 14 December.

Lauder, Adam. 2010. "N.E. Thing Co. Ltd.: From Soft Sell to Soft Skills." In *Byproduct: On the Excess of Embedded Art Practices,* ed. Marisa Jahn, 54–58. Toronto: YYZ Books.

Menger, Pierre-Michel. 2006. "Artistic Labor Markets: Contingent Work, Excess Supply and Occupational Risk Management." In *Handbook of the Economics of Art and Culture Vol. 1,* eds. Victor A. Ginsburgh and David Throsby, 765–811. Amsterdam: North-Holland/Elsevier Science.

Mills, C. Wright. 1951. *White Collar: The American Middle Classes.* New York: Oxford University Press.

Molesworth, Helen. 2000. "House Work and Art Work." *October 92* (Spring):71–97.

Montano, Linda Mary. 1981. *Art in Everyday Life.* Los Angeles, CA: Astro Artz.

Paap, Kirsten. 1997. "Working Class Women, Occupational Realism, and Occupational Choice: Beliefs and Knowledge of Working-Class Women at First Workplace Entrance." MS thesis, University of Wisconsin.

Pink, Daniel. 2005. *A Whole New Mind: Moving from the Information Age to the Conceptual Age.* New York: Riverhead Books.

Raunig, Gerald, Gene Ray, and Ulf Wuggenig, eds. 2011. *Critique of Creativity: Precarity, Subjectivity, and Resistance in the "Creative Industries."* London: MayFly Books.

Schocket, Eric. 2003. "Poor Like Me." *Cabinet 11* (Summer):47–53. www.cabinetmagazine. org/issues/11/poorLikeMe.php (10 December 2011).

Sholette, Gregory. 2011. *Dark Matter: Art and Politics in the Age of Enterprise Culture.* New York: Pluto Press.

Smithsonian Institute. 1969. Unsigned letter,
in Lucy R. Lippard papers, 1940s–2006, bulk
1968–1990. Washington, DC: Archives of
American Art, Smithsonian Institute.

Steyerl, Hito. 2011. "Art as Occupation: Claims
for an Autonomy of Life." *e-flux journal* 30, 12.
www.e-flux.com/journal/art-as-occupation-
claims-for-an-autonomy-of-life-12
(5 January 2012).

Stokes, Leland. 1977. "Effects of Key Figures on
the Occupational Realism of Black Male
Inner-City High School Seniors." PhD diss.
New York: Fordham University.

Styan, J.L. 1981. *Modern Drama in Theory and
Practice, Vol. 1: Realism and Naturalism.*
Cambridge: Cambridge University Press.

Thomas, Mark J. 1976. "Realism and Socioeco-
nomic Status (SES) of Occupational Plans of
Low SES Black and White Male Adolescents."
Journal of Counseling Psychology 23, 1:46–49.

Virno, Paolo. 2004. *A Grammar of the Multitude:
For an Analysis of Contemporary Forms
of Life.* Trans. Isabella Bertoletti,
James Cascaito, and Andrea Casson.
Los Angeles, CA: Semiotext(e).

Weeks, Kathi. 2011. *The Problem with Work:
Feminism, Marxism, Antiwork Politics, and
Postwork Imaginaries.* Durham, NC: Duke
University Press.

Yoon, Bohyun. 2011a. Artist website.
www.bohyunyoon.com (15 November 2011).

———. 2011b. Phone interview with author,
25 November.

NEW CONCEPTS OF WORK AND TIME

Annette Kamp

The world of work is changing. While work in the industrial era was clearly confined in space and time—employees were assembled in well-defined physical places and operated according to well-defined schedules—the boundaries around work today are dissolving at an ever-increasing rate. Work has become boundaryless. As it transcends its traditional delineations, the idea of the "normal working day" or "normal working week" is being gradually effaced. While this allows us to choose our own hours without the structures and limitations of rules and agreements, it also means that all our waking hours are potential working hours.

The eight-hour workday that was fought for throughout the industrial era is still officially the norm. Now, however, the standard is used mainly for calculation purposes and no longer express actual work time spent. In reality, working hours are defined by the nature of the assignment, by solution strategies, and by the level of ambition involved, as well as by individual factors and preferences—all of which add up to "self-determined" hours. These are frequently managed through expectations or demands of a worker's availability, now increasingly accessed and encroached upon by information technologies. Also, expectations of quality, speed, loyalty, and the desire to improve personal employability all play a significant role in our use of time towards work.

In many ways, this kind of boundaryless work does counter the traditional critique of factory work by offering greater autonomy and an opportunity for defining work-life-balance. However, it also leads to new forms of mental strain associated, significantly, with temporality. Social acceleration, lack of time, and the impossibility of solving time-puzzles are the burden of late-modern working life. Whereas the length of our working hours and their position within a twenty-four-hour period traditionally constituted the key to understanding stress factors related to our jobs, stress now seems to originate from different aspects of temporality.

Time as Social Institution

The sociology of time is a broad and fairly heterogeneous field of research. It focuses on a number of classic concepts that help us understand contemporary duration as it relates to work today. Émile Durkheim (1915) was among the first to point out that society renders time naturalized and impersonal. He emphasized that time must be considered a social institution, a set of common rules and norms enabling the coordination of human activity. The regulation of time becomes the key to the cohesion and reproduction of society (Rakoff 2002).

One example is the way the standardization of time as clock time ensured the synchronization required to establish the railway, an infrastructure hugely significant to the development of early capitalism in Europe. As a means of public transportation over great distances, punctuality and predictability were essential. In connection with the development of timetables for the railway, standardized time measurement, Greenwich Mean Time (GMT) was implemented in many greater cities. In fact, GMT was originally known as railway time (Urry 2007). The invention of clockwork, Newtonian physics, and modern economics for that matter, all conspired to create a notion of time as an abstract and independent condition. *Clock time,* perceived as linear and divisible into mathematical units—principally infinitely small segments—is a temporal regime that achieved hegemonic status in the industrial era, particularly in the field of work. Encouraged by standardization, time became a resource to be utilized in the best possible way, where activities are separated and independently streamlined for maximum efficiency; Taylorism and Fordism constitute the very image of such a linear regime. In other words, temporal regimes underpin the transformation of the physical and social world in the sense that significant social inequalities originate from asymmetric opportunities of time and place.

Studies of time, work, and stress show that both the temporal regime and the personal experience of time frame our understanding of and thinking about it, since psychosocial issues are closely connected to the subjective experience of work. Phenomenological approaches that relate to the experience of time help us distinguish between abstract and institutionalized understandings. As we all know, an hour can sometimes feel like an eternity, while at other times we are so busy that we keep glancing at the clock, lest we don't finish before our shift ends. These experiences contrast with situations where we are so consumed by our task that we forget about time altogether, a temporal experience termed *flow* (Csikszentmihalyi 1990, Bloch 2001). Phenomenology uses the term *eigenzeit* to denote the many "personal times" that coexist simultaneously depending on the specific local context (Nowotny 1994). It follows from this line of argument about psychosocial and scientific framings of time that other regimes are in fact possible and that new temporal regimes that compete with clock time may arise.

Time in the Age of Globalization

Several contemporary thinkers point out that a new temporal regime is currently establishing itself. They call attention to how globalization and recent technological developments have propelled a dramatic change in time-space relations, and therefore in time as a social institution. They describe a new temporal regime that is characterized at once by compressed, accelerated, and asynchronous time, a focus on "the now," and by polychronicity, the simultaneous resolution of numerous tasks.

Time is traditionally connected to space in the sense that duration corresponds to a certain distance. Social theorist David Harvey speaks of the "time-space compression" resulting from technological development, particularly (but not exclusively) in relation to information technology (IT) (Harvey 1989). Destinations that were once distant suddenly appear closer; space is shrinking. Time- space relations now seem to be all but suspended. Sociologist John Urry (2000) developed the concept of *instantaneous time* to characterize this new temporal regime in which time and space have effectively been desynchronized. IT exacerbates this by enabling the transmission of information at speeds beyond conscious human perception. Furthermore, the continuing increase in speed and turnover is forever shortening our temporal horizons and fragmenting time. Human activity (work, play, meals, etc.) is becoming increasingly individualized. Now, people follow different rhythms and are rarely present in the same room at the same time. So, what we see is a desynchronization of time-space-activity relations.

Norwegian social anthropologist Thomas Hylland Eriksen provides another interesting characteristic of time in modern society in his book, *Tyranny of the Moment*. His main point is that time now increasingly consists of brief, intense moments—*fast time*—and this fast time is killing the *slow time* in which we are able to immerse ourselves in a task, an experience, or a relation, and work towards long-term goals. Interstices, previously scattered throughout the day, are now being filled with fast time: transportation and waiting, for instance, are now filled with text messaging and e-mails. He believes that such interstices—now being overrun by activities—could have played a significant role in our everyday lives by constituting pauses for reflection and creative distraction.

A New Temporal Regime in Working Life

The question is how this new regime becomes manifest in working life. Globalization and the pervasive use of information technology permeate every aspect of our working lives, in nearly every kind of work. IT transgresses limits in time and space. As previously mentioned, it is, therefore, a precondition for boundaryless work. IT also lets us pack more and more activities into the moment, making multitasking (or to use Hylland Eriksen's expression, *stacking*) ubiquitous. The self-management of time becomes a key skill in its own right and the compression of deadlines becomes an important method of intensification (Allvin 1999, 2006).

Temporary flexibility is central to ongoing process of restructuring. It has become a new demand on workers, a source of precarity, and often compulsory. This development also affects ordinary industrial work, where we see the enforcement of temporal flexibility with the introduction of overtime as required. Krings et al. (2008) mentions an example of a Portuguese factory with subcontractors in India (+five hours) and Brazil (-five hours). In order to coordinate and communicate they are obliged to spread their work over the full twenty-four hours of the day. At a general level, this development leads to the creation of a number of different organizational patterns of working hours: there are groups working long hours (24/7), groups on temporary contracts, and groups spreading their time over several workplaces or working from home.

Additionally, practices such as Just in Time (JIT), which have been important in the movement towards increasingly flexible production, encourage the new temporal regime at work. JIT dictates that everything must happen at just the right time: all commodities must be delivered at the point of need in the right quantity and quality. A major European study of time and work[1] emphasizes how this movement leads to the desire to suspend all "rigidities," rendering the organization flexible according to the "Just in time" principle. JIT can be considered an engine establishing temporal regimes that intensify focus on the moment. At the same time, it indicates that globalization, outsourcing, etc., create a significant need for coordination across different chains of production, just as a greater degree of customer orientation entails a need for synchronization and, thereby, for new temporal structuring of our work. Furthermore, this synchronization must always be improvised according to the needs of the moment.

The continuous rise in individualization and the ensuing desynchronization vis-á-vis increasing demands for coordination across global contexts—a kind of flexible synchronization— will create dilemmas that must be resolved through our self-management of time. Work is increasingly fusing or interfering with the rhythms of private life. We see a parallel interest in the work-life balance, an area that has arisen as an independent field of research and indicates the important role of gender in the experience of temporal structures and the question of priorities in an overall life perspective.[2]

So, it could well be argued that the new temporal regime is currently establishing itself in working life. However, as Paul du Gay emphasizes, describing phenomena as "epochal" is problematic (2003), for example, characterizing the pre-industrial era by cyclic time, the industrial age by clock time, or the postmodern era by instantaneous time. Despite the attractive simplicity of this kind of explanation, he maintains that there is not—nor has there ever been—an absolutely hegemonic temporal regime. Rather, different regimes coexist.

Compounding this, working life is an area where the clock time regime has been particularly elaborated and refined as means of management, and so this regime also persists. Therefore, we often find self-management of time along with the bureaucratic management of time. Employees must navigate through old and new regimes of time management (Kamp et al 2011, Jensen and Westenholz 2004).

Temporal Conflicts

New studies of working life position temporal conflicts as a dominant characteristic of modern work life. These conflicts may concern contradictions between old and new temporal regimes, but also the solution of inherent tensions stemming from the new regime, such as conflicts between fast and slow time. Above all, conflict is managed through the daily negotiation of time, through individual attempts at making various ends meet to complete a complex temporal puzzle. The work of solving the time puzzle may also be conceived as an important factor in the development of the modern epidemic of stress. Certainly, more empirical studies are needed in order to fully understand these dynamics. While existing studies of temporality in work organizations are scarce, four selected examples of such studies in specific fields of labor will give an impression of insights that might be gained from examining temporal conflicts and temporal work.

While temporal regimes is used to describe an overall institutionalized understanding of time and usually refers to a hegemonic order typical for a specific epoch, such as linear time, in these empirical studies more dynamic terms are developed to encompass institutional understandings, produced in local organizational contexts. Examples are the concepts time reference frames and temporal orders.

Oili-Helena Ylijoki and Hans Mätylä (2003) have studied the collective *temporal orders* of academic work to understand the high pace and the shortage of time that dominate this kind of work. The purpose of their study is to understand collective perspectives on time that workers use to explain their work, rather than individual, idiosyncratic notions.

Based on their interviews, Ylijoki and Mätylä have indicated four temporal orders in academic work. *Scheduled time* is that in which externally determined schedules govern teaching and other tasks. Scheduled time is characterized by the need to resolve more and more tasks in ever-decreasing temporal increments, which results in long, fragmented working days characterized by an overriding sense of being pressed for it. Coinciding deadlines simply mean working overtime. At the same time, there is an increasing demand for communication and, therefore, accessibility: online feedback is required in response to external demands. Hence, scheduled time has become increasingly hectic and instantaneous. Ylijoki and Mätylä point out that it relieves the teachers' pressure if scheduled lessons have a linear aspect to them, i.e., a delimited temporal horizon with a beginning and an end. Lessons cause anxiety when perceived as cyclical, recurring and endless. As employees, academics feel they have lost control over their time and wish to regain it in order to carry out their key task of individual research. To resolve this conflict, they use various strategies akin to stealing, borrowing, saving, or buying the time required.

When working with the time puzzle, academics aim to create a certain kind of time that is connected to their identity as professionals: *timeless time*. The term is used to denote time in which employees are consumed by their work, more specifically by what they consider to be their key tasks (reading, writing, thinking, intellectual debate). Employees refer to this kind of time either as something belonging to a distant past or a distant future, i.e., associated with retiring or leaving the department. It has become an almost utopian category.

Most employees are hired on a contractual basis, so *contract time* is associated with workplace insecurity and unpredictability. From a temporal perspective, this leads to a form of discipline where employees feel subject to continuous assessment while constantly being required to apply for funding to ensure future employment. Meanwhile, other employees are never entirely sure who is actually employed at any given moment and hence face a complicated puzzle when planning future work, which in turn leads to yet more feelings of risk-taking and insecurity.

The shortage of time leads to increased pressure on family life, the *personal time* spent in private life. Many worry about their health or about the consequences of neglecting their family. Everyone seeks the ideal work-life balance but few have actually found it. Ylijoki and Mätylä emphasize that these four temporal orders are at odds with one another. Scheduled time, which more or less corresponds to the description of instantaneous time, conflicts with timeless time (slow time). Furthermore, the feelings of insecurity and unpredictability create a sense of risk in their own right as well as functioning dynamically to increase overall pace and intensity. As Hylland Eriksen points out, fast time generally wins: Contract time—as characterized by brief temporal horizons, intensity, the simultaneous resolution of numerous tasks—is dominant overall, and the possibility of timeless time becomes utopian. These pressures and dilemmas leave very little time for pursuing long-term, shared, or community interests.

There are other projects indicating conflicts between different temporal orders, albeit with slightly different approaches. Susan Waterworth (2003), who investigated nurses and their relation-ship to time and work, uses the concept of *temporal reference frameworks* to describe the implicit, socially constructed temporal understandings that serve as underlying expectations forming the basis of employees' time management. Temporal reference frameworks describe an understanding of the amount of time, the pace, synchronization, and sequencing which are considered the norm and hence support action. One important point of the article is that nursing work involves several frameworks and that these may be mutually conflicting.

Among these, *Needing time* is the author's term for time spent with patients in order to know and understand their needs. Here nurses encounter the expectation of duration and undisturbed attention. *Listening time* is a subtype of needing time. This is time spent listening to patient experience and is considered essential for care to lead to cure. Thus needing time is significant in the nurses' own understanding of their profession. However, other temporal orders do interfere. Waterforth has observed two types of interruption: *Wasting time* i.e. useless time where patients, in nurses' opinion, make the wrong of use of them—the bell ringers and those who use them as housekeepers. When third parties such as social workers contact nurses, this, too, is considered wasted time. In contrast, *natural interruptions* stem from things like pagers. While these also interfere with "slow" patient interaction time, they are perceived as a natural and necessary part of the job. These temporal conflicts in their work mean that nurses need to move faster. They literally have to run. They do not have the option of compensating with overtime since they must complete their work by the end of the shift. Through the nurses' attempts to negotiate these temporal conflicts, we understand the kind of pressure and self-intensification that appears in this kind of work.

David Knights & Pamela Odih (2002) carried out a study of the work that takes place in call centers. They too identified conflicting temporal horizons as a key aspect of working conditions. On one hand, this work is characterized by a traditional clock time regime, with great focus on the duration of individual interactions with clients. On the other hand, it also requires employees to be attentive to the emotional qualities of the conversation: the client must experience real human contact. This aspect requires the (temporary) suspension of employees' inner time manager. In this sense, it is comparable to the "needing time" of nursing work in terms of type, if not duration of, the temporal regime.

Leslie Perlow (1999) deals specifically with two aspects of instantaneous time: fragmentation and conflicts between temporal individualization, and the need for synchronicity. She carried out an ethnographic study of a group of computer engineers in order to explain their "long hours culture." She examined patterns of temporal consumption, their effect on the work, and the engineers' own explanations for managing their time. She considers social rhythms to be results of human interactions that simultaneously regulate behavior. In many ways this work is self-organized and flexible. Yet management still gives the orders and establishes reward systems, which significantly influence employee behavior. In other words, this is a working culture supported by management but actively interpreted and put into practice by the employees themselves. The main temporal conflict here lies between the time to carry out what is perceived to be the key task and "interruptions." Although they have a great deal of individual time, it is fragmented and employees cannot necessarily predict their availability. Consequently, many come in early or stay late to have time for their actual work, thus gaining coherent time. Success in this kind of company (i.e., promotion or bonuses) depends on visibility, the ability to adapt to requirements, and to be available, all while agreeing to the demands of management—with no mention of whether these are actually realistic.

Perlow's study indicates how communication and cooperation become interruptions that are neither acknowledged in professionals' understandings of themselves nor by management. Both universes are built on individual concepts of work. Working days are prolonged in an attempt to avoid the temporal fragmentation due to task overload and unsuitable patterns of communication. Perlow indicates that the only way to improve working life is to address the need for synchronicity and community and to acknowledge them as part of the key task.

Simultaneously, we must remain aware of the fact that the multiplicities of temporal orders we encounter in our working lives also characterize our private lives. Our spare time—as illustrated by Julia Everingham's study (2002) of working mothers—is not simply a free zone where time is at our disposal, characterized by cyclical rhythms and daily (or annually) recurring routines: Time for working mothers is best described by several competing temporal orders which cannot easily be combined. In other words, they experience temporal conflicts of "juggling time" just as they do in paid labor. There's "here and now time," where dinner has to be put on the table, conflicts need to be resolved, etc. (This is often a question of multitasking). Then there are long-term tasks and "intense attention time" nurturing children of various ages.

Finally, there is "making time for others time," where mothers must consider all the different rhythms of individual family members, planning and coordinating them to ensure a functional social life for the family as a whole.

Looking Forward: Work to Be Done

The aim of this brief overview is to consider how the thinking and terms introduced by time sociology might be useful in the research of boundaryless work. Boundaryless work may be perceived as enrichment, empowerment, and freedom. Yet, such work is in fact hyper-task-oriented, requiring synchronization, pacing, intensity, endurance, and order. We are asked to be committed, loyal, and even passionate about our work. As the studies show, meeting competing demands and solving time puzzles is hard work. Self-management of time becomes about making work meaningful.

Existing literature points to some key concepts and characteristics of the boundaryless work, which can be useful focal points in the study and description of work strain and stress:

1) The time puzzle of resolving *time conflicts* is a task in and of itself and thus a potential stress element.

2) *Fragmentation of time* and *momentary orientation* are conflicts between fast and slow time, with a shortage of time for immersion as a result of "stacking" (multi-tasking). This results in feeling one never has enough time.

3) *Flexible synchronization* is where the work day is pressured and cut up by the demand for improvised coordination of various tasks.

4) *Increased speed* and *long hours* result in compression and lack of interstices, or pauses.

When it comes to strategies of how to regulate these types of time conflicts or strains in the work place and create a more sustainable work life, the literature offers very little.

Following Lefebvre, Helge Hvid attempts in his study of sustainable social rhythms to offer one possible strategy: He suggests a combination of repetitive structures in time and space along with individual possibilities to differentiate or adjust activities to create new forms or rhythms. His perspective is usefully combined with Hylland Eriksen's more concrete suggestion that we consciously oscillate between *slow* and *fast time.* Whereas Eriksen seeks to retain the elements of slow time, where immersion and the sequential completion of one task at a time is in focus, Hvid suggests a combination of slow and fast time, which is driven by concern over rising strain and the growing desire for development. Unlike Hvid, Eriksen is mostly concerned with how to shield oneself, that is, how to set boundaries against unlimited availability and our fear of missing out on information or not being in the loop. He advocates daring to resist by unplugging and creating pauses. He is not so concerned with how this is actually done, but seen from a work-life perspective, it is evident that possibilities for change lie in formulating shared norms in work communities. This is obviously easier said than done, as part of the problem lies exactly in the disintegration of communities or commons and increased individualization.

In considering strategies with which to counter the strains of work life, commons are central. Shared norms that support the individual are essential to alleviate the increased negotiation of time conflicts, structure work so there are more and better pauses, and create room for immersion and coordination in core work assignments so that the work day is experienced as coherent. Concepts outlined here will need to be supplemented by empirical studies, which will allow us to generate the experience, knowledge, and ideas in response to the time of boundaryless work, and to develop strategies for a good working life.

Notes

[1] Works – Work organization and restructuring in knowledge society. Program under the Sixth Framework Programme of the European Commission, 2005-09.

[2] Although the topic of gender perspectives on time and work certainly merit attention it lies beyond the scope of this text.

References

Allvin, Michael, Gunnar Aronsson, Tom Hagström, Gunn Johansson, and Ulf Lundberg. 2006. *Gränslöst arbete: Socialpsykologiska perspektiv på det nya arbetslivet.* Malmö: Liber.

Allvin, Michael, Per Wiklund, Annika Härenstam, and Gunnar Aronsson. 1999. *Frikopplad eller frånkopplad. Om innebörder och konsekvenser av gränslösa arbeten.* Stockholm: Arbetslivsinstitutet.

Brannen, Julia. 2005. "Time and the negotiation of work-family boundaries: autonomy or illusion." *Time & Society,* 14 (1): 113-131.

Bloch, Charlotte. 2001. *Flow, stress og følelseskultur.* Copenhagen: Samfundslitteratur.

Csikszentmihalyi, Mihaly. 1990. *Flow: The psychology of optimal experience,* New York: Harper Perennial.

Du Gay, Paul. 2003. "The Tyranny of the Epochal: Change, Epochalism and Organizational Reform." *Organization,* 10 (4): 663-684.

Durkheim, Émile. 1915. *The elementary forms of the religious life, a study in religious sociology.* London: G. Allen & Unwin.

Jensen, Torben Elgaard, and Ann Westenholz. 2004. *Identity in the age of the new economy: life in temporary and scattered work practices.* Cheltenham, UK: Edward Elgar Publishing.

Eriksen, Trond Berg. 2004. *Tidens historie.* København: Tiderne Skifter.

Everingham, Christine. 2002. Engendering Time: Gender equity and discourses of workplace flexibility. *Time & Society* 11, (2/3): 335-351.

Harvey, David. 1990. *The condition of postmodernity: an enquiry into the origins of cultural change.* Oxford (England): Blackwell.

Hvid, Helge. 2006. *Arbejde og bæredygtighed.* København: Frydenlund.

Hylland Eriksen, Thomas. 2001. *Øyeblikkets tyranni: rask og langsom tid i informasjonssamfunnet.* Oslo: Aschehoug.

Kamp, Annette, Henrik Lambrecht Lund, and Helge Søndergaard Hvid 2011. "Negotiating time meaning and identity in boundaryless work." Journal of Workplace Learning, 23 (4): 229-243.

Knights, David and Pamela Odih. "'Big brother is watching you!' Call centre surveillance and the time-disciplined subject," in *Social conceptions of time – structure and process in work and everyday life,* ed. Crow, G. and S. Health,144-162. London/Basingstoke, Palgrave Macmillan. 2002

Krings, Bettina-Johanna, Nierling, L. Pedaci. M & M. Piersanti (2008). Working time gender and work-life balance. Works: Thematic Report, 12.7. The European Commission.

Lefebvre, Henri. 2004. *Rhythmanalyses. Space, Time and Everyday Life.* London, Continuum

Nowotny, Helga. 1994. *Time. The modern and postmodern experience*. Cambridge, UK: Polity Press.

Perlow, Leslie A. 1998. "Boundary control: The Social Ordering of Work and Family Time in a High-tech Corporation." *Administrative Science Quarterly*, 43 (2): 328-357.

———— 1999. "The time famine." *Administrative Science Quarterly* 44, 1 (Mar., 1999):57-81.

Rakoff, Todd D. 2002. *Time for every purpose: law and balance of life* Cambridge, Mass: Harvard University Press.

Urry, John. 2005. *Sociology beyond societies: mobilities for the twenty-first century*. London: Routledge.

Urry, John. 2007. Mobilities. Cambridge, UK: Polity.

Ylijoki, O. and Mätylä, H. 2003. "Conflicting Time Perspectives in Academic Work." *Time & Society* 12, (1): 55-78.

Westenholz, Ann. 2006. "Identity, times and work." *Time and Society*, 15 (1): 33-55.

Works – Work organisation and restructuring in knowledge society. *Programme under the Sixth Framework. Programme of the European Commission.*
http://www.workinglives.org/research-themes/restructuring/work-organisation-and-restructuring-in-the-knowledge-society-works.cfm.

8 HOURS

8 HOURS

8 HOURS

LABOR

RECREATION

REST

THE PROBLEM WITH WORK

Kathi Weeks

Introduction

> Though women do not complain of the power of husbands,
> each complains of her own husband, or of the husbands of
> her friends. It is the same in all other cases of servitude, at
> least in the commencement of the emancipatory movement.
> The serfs did not at first complain of the power of their lords,
> but only of their tyranny.
>
> JOHN STUART MILL, *THE SUBJECTION OF WOMEN*

> One type of work, or one particular job, is contrasted with
> another type, experienced or imagined, within the present
> world of work; judgments are rarely made about the world
> of work as presently organized as against some other way
> of organizing it.
>
> C. WRIGHT MILLS, *WHITE COLLAR*

Why do we work so long and so hard? The mystery here is not
that we are required to work or that we are expected to devote
so much time and energy to its pursuit, but rather that there is not
more active resistance to this state of affairs. The problems with
work today—my focus will be on the United States—have to do
with both its quantity and its quality and are not limited to the
travails of any one group. Those problems include the low wages
in most sectors of the economy; the unemployment, underemploy-
ment, and precarious employment suffered by many workers; and
the overwork that often characterizes even the most privileged

forms of employment—after all, even the best job is a problem when it monopolizes so much of life. To be sure, if we were only resigned to such conditions, there would be no puzzle. What is perplexing is less the acceptance of the present reality that one must work to live than the willingness to live for work. By the same token, it is easy to appreciate why work is held in such high esteem, but considerably less obvious why it seems to be valued more than other pastimes and practices.

Work is not just an economic practice. Indeed, that every individual is required to work, that most are expected to work for wages or be supported by someone who does, is a social convention and disciplin ary apparatus rather than an economic necessity. That every individual must not only do some work but more often a lifetime of work, that individuals must not only work but become workers, is not necessary to the production of social wealth. The fact is that this wealth is collectively not individually produced, despite the persistence of an older economic imaginary that links individual production directly to consumption.[1] Indeed, as Postone observes, "on a deep, systemic level, production is not for the sake of consumption" (1996, 184). The relationship may appear direct and incontrovertible, but it is in fact highly mediated: the goal of neither party in the work relation is consumption; one seeks surplus value, and the other income. The normative expectation of waged work as an individual responsibility has more to do with the socially mediating role of work than its strictly productive function (150). Work is the primary means by which individuals are integrated not only into the economic system, but also into social, political, and familial modes of cooperation. That individuals should work is fundamental to the basic social contract; indeed, working is part of what is supposed to transform subjects into the independent individuals of the liberal imaginary, and for that reason, is treated as a basic obligation of citizenship. (The fact that the economy's health is dependent on a permanent margin of unemployment is only one of the more notorious problems with this convention.) Dreams of individual accomplishment and desires to contribute to the common good become firmly attached to waged work, where they can be hijacked to rather different ends: to produce neither individual riches nor social wealth, but privately appropriated surplus value. The category of the work society is meant to signify not only the centrality of work, but also its broad field of social relevance (see, for example, Beck 2000).

Work Values

The category of the work society refers not just to the socially mediating and subjectively constitutive roles of work but to the dominance of its values. Challenging the present organization of work requires not only that we confront its reification and depoliticization but also its normativity and moralization. Work is not just defended on grounds of economic necessity and social duty; it is widely understood as an individual moral practice and collective ethical obligation. Traditional work values—those that preach the moral value and dignity of waged work and privilege such work as an essential source of individual growth, selffulfill-ment, social recognition, and status—continue to be effective in encouraging and rationalizing the long hours US workers are supposed to dedicate to waged work and the identities they are expected to invest there. This normalizing and moralizing ethic of work should be very familiar to most of us; it is, after all, routinely espoused in managerial discourse, defended in the popular media, and enshrined in public policies. The ethic's productivist values are promoted on both the political Right and Left, from employers seeking the most able and tractable workers, and politicians intent on moving women from welfare to waged work, to parents and educators eager to prepare their children or students to embrace the values that might best ensure their future economic security and social achievement.

Let me be clear: to call these traditional work values into question is not to claim that work is without value. It is not to deny the necessity of productive activity or to dismiss the likelihood that, as William Morris describes it, there might be for all living things "a pleasure in the exercise of their energies" (1999, 129). It is, rather, to insist that there are other ways to organize and distribute that activity and to remind us that it is also possible to be creative outside the boundaries of work. It is to suggest that there might be a variety of ways to experience the pleasure that we may now find in work, as well as other pleasures that we may wish to discover, cultivate, and enjoy. And it is to remind us that the willingness to live for and through work renders subjects supremely functional for capitalist purposes. But before the work society can be publicized and raised as a political problem, we need to understand the forces—including the work ethic—that promote our acceptance of and powerful identification with work and help to make it such a potent object of desire and privileged field of aspiration.

Feminism has its own tendencies toward the mystification and moralization of work and has reproduced its own version of this famed ethic. Consider two of the dominant feminist remedies for the gender divisions and hierarchies of waged and unwaged work. One strategy, popular with at least some feminists of both the first and second waves, is to more or less accept the lesser value accorded to unwaged domestic labor and seek to secure women's equal access to waged work. Waged work would be women's ticket out of culturally mandated domesticity. While recognizing the importance of the ongoing struggle to secure equal employment opportunities for women, I want to argue that subjecting feminism's own idealization of waged work to critical scrutiny remains an important task as well. Confronting the present organization of waged labor and its values is especially urgent in the wake of the 1996 welfare reform debate and resulting legislation. Certainly the attack on poor women that was perpetrated in the name of the work ethic should inspire the reconsideration and reinvention of feminist perspectives on waged work—its ever-shifting realities and its long-standing values.

A second feminist strategy concentrates on efforts to revalue unwaged forms of household-based labor, from housework to caring work. Certainly making this socially necessary labor visible, valued, and equitably distributed remains a vital feminist project as well. The problem with both of these strategies—one focused on gaining women's entry into all forms of waged work and the other committed to gaining social recognition of, and men's equal responsibility for, unwaged domestic work—is their failure to challenge the dominant legitimating discourse of work. On the contrary, each approach tends to draw upon the language and sentiments of the traditional work ethic to win support for its claims about the essential dignity and special value of women's waged or unwaged labor.[2] How might feminism contest the marginalization and underestimation of unwaged forms of reproductive labor, without trading on the work ethic's mythologies of work? Feminists, I suggest, should focus on the demands not simply or exclusively for more work and better work, but also for less work; we should focus not only on revaluing feminized forms of unwaged labor but also challenge the sanctification of such work that can accompany or be enabled by these efforts.

The question is, then, how to struggle against both labor's misrecognition and devaluation on the one hand, and its metaphysics and moralism on the other hand. The refusal of work, a concept drawn from the autonomous Marxist tradition, will help to focus the analysis on the question of work's meaning and value. In contrast to some other types of Marxism that confine their critique of capitalism to the exploitation and alienation of work without attending to its overvaluation, this tradition offers a more expansive model of critique that seeks to interrogate at once capitalist production and capitalist (as well as socialist) productivism. From the perspective of the refusal of work, the problem with work cannot be reduced to the extraction of surplus value or the degradation of skill, but extends to the ways that work dominates our lives. The struggle against work is a matter of securing not only better work, but also the time and money necessary to have a life outside work. Although there are a number of important analyses of the most exploited forms of waged and unwaged work performed by workers both in the United States and beyond its borders, the larger systems of labor and especially the values that help sustain them are often insufficiently theorized, leaving one to conclude that all of our work-related goals would be met and the dominant work values justified if only such work were to resemble more closely the employment conditions at the middle and upper reaches of the labor hierarchy. The theory and practice of the refusal of work insists that the problem is not just that work cannot live up to the ethic's idealized image, that it neither exhibits the virtues nor delivers the meaning that the ethic promises us in exchange for a lifetime of work, but perhaps also the ideal itself.

Post-Fordism and the Work Ethic

The political and economic developments associated with post-Fordism exert some new pressures on the work ethic. Current trends suggest that our attitudes toward work are of increasing importance to the continued viability of contemporary modes of work and their governance. One could argue that with neoliberal restructuring and the shift in the balance of power between capital and labor that it signals, the coercive inducements to hard work and long hours are often sufficient to deliver manageable workers to the labor market. Indeed, the increasing mobility of capital in comparison to the ongoing restrictions on labor's movement alters the political landscape. The threat of job loss attributed to the pressures of global competition puts workers on the defensive, while the contraction of social welfare provisions further enforces individuals' dependence on the wage relation. The precarious position that so many workers find themselves in echoes that of Weber's Puritan, whose restless anxiety and uncertainty kept his nose to the grindstone.[3]

In such a climate, one could conclude that capital is—to recall Weber's claim about an earlier period—back "in the saddle" (1958,

282, n. 108) laborers than their sacrifice and submission, seeking to enlist their creativity and their relational and affective capacities. It is not obedience that is prized, but commitment; employees are more often expected to adopt the perspectives of managers rather than simply yield to their authority (Bunting 2004, 110). Whereas Fordism demanded from its core workers a lifetime of compliance with work discipline, post-Fordism also demands of many of its workers flexibility, adaptability, and continual reinvention.[4] If originally the work ethic was the means by which already disciplined workers were delivered to their exploitation, it serves a more directly productive function today: where attitudes themselves are productive, a strong work ethic guarantees the necessary level of willing commitment and subjective investment. Especially in the context of service work and work with an affective or communications component, the individual's attitude and emotional state are considered crucial skills, along with empathy and sociability.[5] Indeed, the very distinction between a worker's skills and attitudes becomes difficult to sustain, since, as Robin Leidner notes, "the willingness and capacity of workers to manipulate and project their attitudes in the organization's interest are central to their competence on the job" (1996, 46). Thus, Doug Henwood claims, "employer surveys reveal that bosses care less about their employees' candlepower than they do about 'character'—by which they mean self-discipline, enthusiasm, and responsibility" (1997, 22).[6] As Arlie Hochschild observes in her groundbreaking study of interactive service sector work, "seeming to 'love the job' becomes part of the job; and actually trying to love it, and to enjoy the customers, helps the worker in this effort" (1983, 6). Indeed, now more than ever, "workers are expected to be the architects of their own better exploitation" (Henwood 1997, 22).

But it is not only a matter of what kind of labor power is often sought. When workers are given more responsibility and more discretion, and particularly when the job involves providing services and instilling in clients and customers certain kinds of emotional or affective states, the workers' performance is more difficult both to measure and to monitor. How does one determine an individual employee's contribution to increasingly cooperative labor processes, particularly those that draw on workers' affective, cognitive, and communicative capacities? ("This call may be monitored for purposes of quality assurance"—but it probably is not.) When individual contributions to collective production processes are more difficult to discern, employers focus on measuring what they can, increasingly resorting to proximate measures. Personality testing is thus on the rise as one kind of proxy for behavioral assessment, and in this way, "the emphasis becomes the total behavior of the individual rather than the specifically 'productive' behavior" (Townley 1989, 106). Putting in long hours can also be used as an indication of commitment, which can in turn be a signal of productivity. A worker's devotion to work serves as a sign of his or her capacities just as it once served as a sign of his or her status among the elect. Strong work values are thus increasingly highlighted in management discourses as a significant remedy to the new problems of surveillance simply because they render it less necessary. Thus, we see a growing trend in the United States and elsewhere to both select and evaluate workers on the basis of their attitudes, motivation, and behavior. This is becoming increasingly the case not just for workers in the higher-paid reaches of the employment hierarchy but for those in the lower-paid levels as well: these criteria are being used on white-, pink-, and increasingly blue-collar employees, in both the industrial and service sectors (92; see also Ehrenreich 2001).

Managing Post-Fordist Independence: Being Professional

These post-Taylorist labor processes pose new challenges for management efforts to construct workers who are, to recall an earlier discussion, both independent and dependent, both autonomously creative and responsive to command. The crude subjectification of Taylor's Schmidt is guided now by a myriad of management theories and a major industry that aids in the manufacture of productive corporate cultures: the relatively simple industrial psychology of the Fordist era had been remade into the complex art of cultural fashioning and emotional engineering typical of many managerial regimes today. The problem for many employers is one of encouraging employee self-development, but only as a "human resource"—or, as some critics of this logic of managerial control describe it, "encouraging autonomous employees to use their alleged independence to express their resourcefulness as well as to submit themselves to continuous self-scrutiny and audit in the name of accountability" (Costea, Crump, and Amiridis, 2008, 673-74). The impoverishment of this conception of individual development, tethered as it is to a mandate to produce value, is made painfully clear in the management guru Tom Peters's description of work as an opportunity to maximize one's chances of future employment, as what can "teach you new skills, gain you new expertise, develop new capabilities, grow your colleague set, and constantly reinvent you as a brand" (1997,94).

Just as the Protestant ethic encouraged workers to treat their work as if it were a calling, today one noteworthy management technique involves asking workers to approach their work as if it were a career. Taylor asked the iconic industrial laborer Schmidt if he were the "high priced man" who embodied the Fordist work ethic of social mobility; the comparable injunction for many postindustrial service workers is to "be professional." The discourse of professionalism today enjoys a wide application, serving as a disciplinary mechanism to manage the affects and attitudes of a service-based workforce that is less amenable to direct supervision. A brief excavation of the category's purposes and applications from the industrial to the postindustrial labor orders can suggest the significance of the increasingly ubiquitous deployment of the figure of the professional and its codes of comportment.

The category of professional work was once defined narrowly. Confined to those jobs that were subject to a measure of self-regulation, required specialized knowledge, and involved a relatively high degree of discretion and judgment, the label was traditionally reserved for the fields of law, medicine, and the clergy. To be a professional was to have a career—a calling—as opposed to a "mere" job: "To the professional person his work becomes his life. Hence the act of embarking upon a professional career is similar in some respects to entering a religious order" (Greenwood 1966, 17). The professional's relationship to his or her calling entailed an erosion of the temporal boundaries between work and life, and a different calibration of the qualities of emotional investment between the times and spaces of work and life outside it. As Lisa Disch and Jean O'Brien observe in the case of professorial labor, the professional regards him or herself as incommensurable and, therefore, is willing to do what needs doing rather than only what he or she is paid to do (2007, 149). Professional socialization has always served as a disciplinary mechanism, one that can induce the effort and commitment, entitlement and identification, and—perhaps above all—the self-monitoring considered necessary to a profession's reproduction as such.

The expansion of the professional strata and of the ideology of professionalism was something C. Wright Mills noted in his early anticipation of the changes in work wrought by the move to a postindustrial labor order and the new ways that subjectivity is put to work in white-collar occupations. Whereas the term once suggested a certain mastery of a field of knowledge linked to a specific skill and expertise, increasingly the mastery that a professional is expected to achieve is over what Mills called "the personality." In other words, whereas the high-priced man of Taylor's narrative was required to discipline his physical efforts, today's professional is supposed to gain control over his or her thoughts, imagination, relationships, and affects. Certainly one purpose of this is to promote the kind of self-discipline and subjective investment long associated with being a professional. And because, like the high-priced man, the professional "wears a badge of prestige" (C. Mills 1951, 138), the practice of hailing a wide range of workers as professionals also serves to cash in on the term's cachet and encourage employees to identify with jobs further up the labor hierarchy. To recall Weber's description of the Protestant work ethic, according to which all waged workers were expected to approach their work industriously as if it were a calling, those in low-waged service-sector jobs under post-Fordism are asked to approach their work professionally as if it were a "career." This professionalization of work, the expansion of what is considered a profession and, more important, the number of workers who are expected to "be professional" is one way this disciplinary subjectification is extended both up and down the labor hierarchy in a post-Taylorist age.

Professionalization in this broader application is more about style, affect, and attitude than about the content of the work. Mills notes that "white-collar workers" "claims to prestige are expressed, as their label implies, by their style of appearance" (241). In contrast to the uniforms typically required of blue-collar workers, white-collar employees wear their own clothes, mass-produced and standardized though they may be, both at work and at home. This is, Mills observes, reflected in the amount of money that white-collar workers, especially women, spend on clothes. As the studies of two very different contemporary workforces each affirms, the "collar" metaphor has always been about clothes, and clothes in turn are key signifiers of the professional. Carla Freeman's (2000) study of pink-collar office workers in the Caribbean focuses on how the workers were encouraged to identify themselves as professionals, an identification that centered crucially on styles of clothing. This was a source of many pleasures, even or particularly when there was little else about the work that was comparably satisfying. In this case, the discourse of professionalism links the practices and identities of production with those of consumption; indeed, that is part of the attraction of professionalized work, one of the ways that this ideology of the professional promotes consent to and identification with work. Linking professional status and identity to the practices of consumption taps into the many ways that style and dress can serve as statements of individuality, markers of status, objects of pleasure, and sites of aspiration. The professional look, and the time and resources necessary to achieve it, tie us not only economically and socially but also aesthetically and affectively to work. What Andrew Ross dubs the "no-collar" nonconformist mentality of a higher-paid technoscientific knowledge and informational workforce in the United States is signaled by a fashion style quite explicitly opposed to the dress codes of the organizational white-collar worker of high Fordism. Indeed, the creativity and individuality of this no-collar style serves to capture visually the ideal of work that the post-Fordist work ethic celebrates. The carefully crafted theatricality of style signifies the kind of creativity, risk, and iconoclasm that these Internet industries try to sell to both customers and their own workers, to both their "external" and "internal" clients (see Ross 2003, 3, 32, 50).

The workers described in both Freeman's and Ross's accounts used clothes and style as a way to distinguish their employment sector from others (as pink-collar rather than blue-collar, or as no-collar in contrast to white-collar) and, by the same token, to display their status as individuals within that setting rather than merely as members of a "collared" class fraction. But as Hochschild notes in her study of flight attendants, another iconic pink-collar labor force, by defending the intensive managerial control over the workers' appearance through "continuous reference to the need to be 'professional,'" the standardized results may be imbued with honor and the aura of autonomy, but they nonetheless remain highly regulated.[7] According to the industry's standard of professionalism, "the flight attendant who most nearly meets the appearance code ideal is therefore 'the most professional.'" Consequently, she observes, "for them a 'professional' flight attendant is one who has completely accepted the rules of standardization" (1983, 103).

Today the term "professional" refers more to a prescribed attitude toward any work than the status of some work. To act like a professional—to be professional in one's work—calls for subjective investment in and identification with work, but also a kind of affective distancing from it. A professional invests his or her person in the job but does not "take it personally" when dealing with difficult co-workers, clients, patients, students, passengers, or customers. As an ideal of worker subjectivity, this requires not just the performance of a role, but a deeper commitment of the self, an immersion in and identification not just with work, but with work discipline. The popular injunction to "be professional," to cultivate a professional attitude, style, and persona, serves as one way that the autonomy, especially of immaterial workers, can be manageri-ally constituted up and down the post-Fordist labor hierarchy.

The importance of the (work) ethic persists under the conditions of post-Fordism, as does its vulnerability. The ability of work to harness desires for a life beyond work depends, perhaps now more than ever, on the power of the work ethic. The ethic's consistent prescriptions for our identification with and constant devotion to work, its elevation of work as the rightful center of life, and its affirmation of work as an end in itself all help to produce the kinds of workers and the laboring capacities adequate to the contemporary regime of accumulation and the specific modes of social labor in which it invests. But the changes in the labor processes that make work values more important to capital may also render them less plausible. With each reconstitution of the work ethic, more is expected of work: from an epistemological reward in the deliverance of certainty, to a socioeconomic reward in the possibility of social mobility, to an ontological reward in the promise of meaning and selfactualization. Indeed, for the anxious Protestant of Weber's account, the quality of work and quantity of wages, the nature of the concrete task and the amount of income it earned, were less relevant than the level of effort the worker applied. Today, in contrast, both the quality of the labor process and the quantity of its material rewards are relevant to the ability of the discourse to deliver on its new ideals of work.

With so much at stake, weighed down with so many expectations, it is no wonder that the ethical discourse of work is becoming ever more abstracted from the realities of many jobs. Within the two-tiered labor market, we find new modes of "over-valorized work" at one end of the labor hierarchy and "devalorized work" at the other (Peterson 2003, 76). Making labor flexible results in an increase of part-time, temporary, casual, and precarious forms of work. At one end, as Stanley Aronowitz and William DiFazio note, "the quality and the quantity of paid labor no longer justify—if they ever did—the underlying claim derived from religious sources that has become the basis of contemporary social theory and social policy: the view that paid work should be the core of personal identity" (1994, 302). At the other end of the labor hierarchy, work is expected to be the whole of life, colonizing and eclipsing what remains of the social. At the same time, the work ethic is more insistently—and perhaps desperately—defended. "Never," André Gorz observes, "has the 'irreplaceable,' 'indispensable' function of labour as the source of 'social ties,' 'social cohesion,' 'integration,' 'socialization,' 'personalization,' 'personal identity' and meaning been invoked so obsessively as it has since the day it became unable any longer to fulfill *any* of these functions" (1999, 57). Today we hear once again about the potentially drastic consequences of a weakening work ethic among yet another generation whose members, it is feared, will fail to be successfully interpellated. Given the work ethic's internal instabilities, we might conclude that its advocates and promoters have cause to be concerned. Where attitudes are productive, an insubordination to the work ethic; a skepticism about the virtues of self-discipline for the sake of capital accumulation; an unwillingness to cultivate, simply on principle, a good "professional" attitude about work; and a refusal to subordinate all of life to work carry a new kind of subversive potential. My claims are that, given its role, the work ethic *should* be contested, and, due to its instabilities, it *can* be contested.

The Refusal of Work

The refusal of work as theory and practice emerges out of these methodological commitments and areas of conceptual focus. As an important slogan in the Italian social movements of the 1960s and 1970s, the refusal of work is a fundamental ground of autonomist Marxism's critical analysis and political strategy, a critical element of the project of autonomy characterized above. At one level a clear expression of the immediate desire experienced by working people around the world, the refusal of work has been developed by autonomists into a more variegated concept, one that encompasses several distinct critical approaches and strategic agendas.

The concept's force, it should be acknowledged, comes from a prior understanding of the place of work in the critical analysis of capitalist social formations. That is, fundamental to the refusal of work as analysis and strategy is a definition of capitalism that highlights not the institution of private property, but rather the imposition and organization of work. After all, from a worker's perspective, earning wages—not accumulating capital—is the primary concern. The wage system remains the dominant mechanism by which individuals are integrated, either directly or indirectly, into the capitalist mode of economic cooperation. Cleaver therefore defines capital as "*a social system based on the imposition of work through the commodity-form*"; it is a system built upon the subordination of life to work (2000, 82). Diane Elson's reading of Marx is helpful in fleshing this out. As she explains Marx's theory of value, it is best understood not as a labor theory of value but as a value theory of labor. In other words, the purpose of the analysis is not to prove the existence of exploitation or to explain prices; the point is not to grasp the process by which value is constituted by labor, but rather to fathom how laboring practices are organized, shaped, and directed by the capitalist pursuit of value. "My argument," Elson writes, "is that the *object* of Marx's theory of value was labour" (1979, 123). Whereas socialist modernization and socialist humanism each imagine the possibility of a postcapitalist society in terms of the realization of the constitutive power of labor, as a matter of grasping the centrality of labor to social life or to individual existence, in this alternative reading of Marx, "labor's constitutive centrality to social life characterizes capitalism and forms the ultimate ground of its abstract mode of domination" (Postone 1996,361). The crucial point and the essential link to the refusal of work is that work—not private property, the market, the factory, or the alienation of our creative capacities—is understood to be the primary basis of capitalist relations, the glue that holds the system together. Hence, any meaningful transformation of capitalism requires substantial change in the organization and social value of work.

Thus, unlike the modernization model, the autonomist tradition focuses on the critique of work under capitalism, which includes but cannot be reduced to the critique of its exploitation. In contrast to the humanists, who also critique work, autonomous Marxists call not for a liberation of work but for a liberation from work (Virno and Hardt 1996, 263). In their insistence on replacing one slogan of worker militancy, "the right to work," with a new one, "the refusal of work," the autonomists certainly follow in the foot-steps of Marx—the Marx who, for example, insisted that freedom depended on the shortening of the working day. But perhaps a more appropriate precursor is Marx's son-in-law, Paul Lafargue. Leszek Kolakowski's description of Lafargue as the proponent of "a hedonist Marxism" only makes this genealogy all the more appropriate (1978, 141–48). Of course, Kolakowski intended his label as an insult, meant to signal Lafargue's naiveté and lack of seriousness, but it is also a fitting classification for a Marxist tradi-tion committed to the refusal of work and open to the possibilities of a postwork future. In *The Right to Be Lazy*, Lafargue takes on the capitalist morality that "curses the flesh of the worker" and seeks to reduce the worker's needs, pleasures, and passions (1898, 3–4). But the immediate target is the 1848 right-towork rhetoric of the French proletariat, which, he complains, echoes and reinforces this ethic of workevidence to Lafargue that the proletariat has "allowed itself to be seduced by the dogma of work" (8). In a ploy reminiscent of Marx's insistence that alienated labor is the cause of private property, that the proletarians themselves recreate the system through their continued participation, Lafargue admonishes the French workers rather than the bourgeoisie for the shortcomings of capitalist production. "All individual and society [*sic*] misery," he insists, "takes its origin in the passion of the proletariat for work" (8). So, for example, when the manufacturers consume luxuries in excess or when they attempt to build obsolescence into their products, they should not be blamed; they are only trying to satisfy "the crazy desire for work on the part of the employees" (31). Because of this strange and furious mania for work, the workers do not demand enough: "The proletarians have got it into their heads to hold the capitalists to ten hours of factory work." That, he insists, is the great mistake: "Work must be forbidden, not imposed" (37). One of the most striking elements of the text is Lafargue's rather extravagant refusal to rehabilitate nonwork by recourse to productivist values. He disdains the "capitalist creed of usefulness" and claims that once the working day is reduced to three hours, workers can begin "to practice the virtues of laziness" (41, 32). Certainly his passionate tribute to "O, Laziness, mother of the arts and the noble virtues" (41) offers a pointed contrast to seemingly more serious interpreters of Marx like Kolakowski, who supports a very different reading. Although it is true, Kolakowski concedes, that Marx did support shorter working hours, this was not to give the worker more time for "carefree consumption" as Lafargue suggests, but rather, as Kolakowski reassures us in a language resonant of more traditional and respectable virtues, "more time for free creative activity" (1978, 148).

Despite Lafargue's provocative tribute to the merits of laziness, the refusal of work is not in fact a rejection of activity and creativity in general or of production in particular. It is not a renunciation of labor *tout court*, but rather a refusal of the ideology of work as highest calling and moral duty, a refusal of work as the necessary center of social life and means of access to the rights and claims of citizenship, and a refusal of the necessity of capitalist control of production. It is a refusal, finally, of the asceticism of those—even those on the Left—who privilege work over all other pursuits, including "carefree consumption." Its immediate goals are presented as a reduction of work, in terms of both hours and social importance, and a replacement of capitalist forms of organization by new forms of cooperation. It is not only a matter of refusing exploited and alienated labor, but of refusing "work itself as the principle of reality and rationality" (Baudrillard 1975, 141). In this sense, "work which is liberated is liberation from work" (Negri 1991, 165). Rather than conceive the refusal of work narrowly, in terms of a specific set of actions—including strikes or slowdowns, demands for shorter hours or expanded opportunities for participation, and movements for improved support for or altered conditions of reproductive work—the phrase is, I suggest, best understood in very broad terms as designating a general political and cultural movement—or, better yet, as a potential mode of life that challenges the mode of life now defined by and subordinated to work.

The refusal of work can be broken down, analytically if not practically, into two processes, one that is essentially critical in its aims and another that is more fundamentally reconstructive in its objectives. The first of these, the negative process, is what is most readily conveyed by the word "refusal" and includes the critique of and rebellion against the present system of work and its values. If the system of waged labor is a crucial cultural and institutional mechanism by which we are linked to the mode of production, then the refusal of work poses a potentially substantial challenge to this larger apparatus. But the refusal of work, as both activism and analysis, does not simply pose itself against the present organization of work; it should also be understood as a creative practice, one that seeks to reappropriate and reconfigure existing forms of production and reproduction (see Vercellone 1996, 84). This is the special twofold nature of the refusal of work upon which Negri insists (2005, 269–74). The word "refusal" may be unfortunate in the sense that it does not immediately convey the constructive element that is so central to autonomist thought. Negri describes the refusal of work as both a struggle against the capitalist organization of work and a process of selfvalorization, a form of "invention-power" (274). Rather than a goal in itself, "the refusal of work and authority, or really the refusal of voluntary servitude, is the *beginning* of liberatory politics" (Hardt and Negri 2000, 204; emphasis added).

The refusal of work thus comprises at once a movement of exit and a process of invention. The refusal can make time and open spaces—both physical and conceptual—within which to construct alternatives. Rather than a simple act of disengagement that one completes, the refusal is, in this sense, a process, a theoretical and practical movement that aims to effect a separation through which we can pursue alternative practices and relationships. "Beyond the simple refusal, or as part of that refusal," Hardt and Negri argue, "we need also to construct a new mode of life and above all a new community" (204). Paolo Virno develops this same idea through the concepts of exodus and exit: "The 'exit' modifies the conditions within which the conflict takes place, rather than presupposes it as an irremovable horizon; it changes the context within which a problem arises, rather than deals with the problem by choosing one or another of the alternative solutions already on offer" (1996, 199). In this sense, refusal, like exodus or exit, is an "*engaged withdrawal* (or founding leave-taking)" (197), a creative practice as opposed to a merely defensive stance. The passage from the negative moment of refusal to its constructive moment of exit and invention marks the shift from a reactive gesture of retreat to an active affirmation of social innovation. According to this reading, the refusal of work serves not as a goal, but as a path—a path of separation that creates the conditions for the construction of subjects whose needs and desires are no longer as consistent with the social mechanisms within which they are supposed to be mediated and contained. This is why, in contrast to both modern-ization and humanist Marxisms, Negri locates in the refusal of work not just the symptoms of exploitation and alienation, but a measure of freedom (2005, 273). The defection enacted through the refusal of work is not predicated upon what we lack or cannot do, it is not the path of those with nothing to lose but their chains; it is predicated instead on our "latent wealth, on an abundance of possibilities" (Virno 1996, 199).

By this account, the negative and positive moments of refusal can be distinguished analytically, but not isolated practically. Rather than the traditional two-stage model that posits a radical break between the transition, conceived as a negative process of dismantling, and communism, imagined as the positive construction of an alternative, the logic of this analysis suggests the value of a more substantial break between the present logic of capital and the transition—seen in this case as a process by which a different future can be constructed. That is, this formulation of the relationship between means and ends indicates the importance of pursuing more radical strategies that attempt a more significant break with the present. In this way we might also better understand the militancy of the strategy—the call to refuse and transform the present system of work, rather than simply to reconsider or renegotiate a few of its terms and conditions. Although the immoderate character of the phrase "refusal of work" may strike us today as naive or impractical, if we consider such strategies as laboratories—both conceptual and practical—in which different subjectivities can be constituted and paths to alternative futures opened, the utopian aspect of the refusal of work, its insistence that we struggle toward and imagine the possibilities of substantial social change, is essential.

Epilogue: A Life beyond Work

> The question of the right to a full life has to be divorced completely from the question of work.
> JAMES BOGGS. *THE AMERICAN REVOLUTION*

I want to end with two brief clarifications of my larger argument, followed by one supplement to it. The latter consists of a way to conceive the demands for basic income and shorter hours as elements of a broader political project. But before we get there, two aspects of the analysis call for further explication: first, the prescription of a politics (a postwork politics) to counter the power of an ethic (the work ethic); and second, the defense of limited demands as tools for radical change. The one requires some attention to the distinction between politics and ethics that the analysis has only presumed so far; the other concerns the specific understanding of the relationship between reform and revolution that informs the argument.

Politics and Change

I will begin here: why counter the power of the work ethic with a postwork politics and not with a postwork ethic? One could, after all, imagine the contours of a postwork ethic as something distinct from a postwork morality—a matter, to cite Virno's formulation, of "common practices, usages and customs, not the dimension of the must-be" (2004, 49). Deleuze marks the distinction this way: ethics are immanent to different modes of existence, whereas morals are imposed from above (1988, 23). But despite the ways that the terrain of ethics can be helpfully distinguished from that of traditional morality I am still more interested in the possibilities of a politics than in the construction of a counterethic. Certainly the relationship between ethics and politics is a close one, with both modes of thinking and acting focusing on the question of how we might live together, both operating in private and public spheres and suffusing at once structures and subjectivities. Indeed, postwork politics and postwork ethics are mutually constitutive, each part of what produces and sustains the other. Nonetheless, because ethics remains more closely tethered than politics to the register of individual belief and choice, my argument prioritizes politics, understood in terms of collective action and fields of institutional change, over ethics, with its focus on practices of the self and encounters with the other. My preference for political rather than ethical remedies might then be understood as a polemical defense of a certain kind of structuralist impulse, a way to keep our focus trained on collective rather than individual action and on the task of changing the institutions and discourses that frame individual lives and relations.

Whereas the distinction between politics and ethics remains meaningful to me for the purposes of this project, the distinction between reform and revolution—which my affirmation of utopian visions together with my defense of restricted demands, would seem to confound—is more problematic. Of course the reform-revolution division has a long, storied history within Marxism, and the status of wage demands has often served as one of its traditional staging grounds. The choice of either reform or revolution continues to haunt some of the conflicts between anticapitalist pragmatists and radicals today, even if the terms of such debates are not posed as boldly as they were in the period of the Second International. From one still-familiar perspective, the idea of revolution is at best a distraction and at worst a diversion from the struggle for change; from the other, the commitment to reform represents a capitulation to the existing terms of that struggle. Whereas one supposedly betrays the present to a far-off future, the other is accused of sacrificing the future to the exigencies of a narrowly conceived present.

The utopian demand is meant to cut through such formulas. It is not that the utopian demand is a reformist alternative to the manifesto's revolutionary program, but that the demand refuses this traditional dichotomy. The radical potential of such relatively modest demands lies in two qualities that we reviewed in the previous chapter: their directionality and performativity. Selma James evokes the first of these in terms of the difference between preparing to lose the fight against capital, but with the hope of salvaging some concessions from the wreck of that defeat, and striving to succeed, while at the same time recognizing that" in struggling to *win*, plenty can be gained along the way (Dalla Costa and James 1973, 1). The demands that emerge out of the latter strategy are likely to be utopian demands, demands that, at their best, simultaneously speak to and direct us beyond the confines of the present. Antonio Negri alludes to the second quality in his claim about the potential generativity of reforms. As he explains it, the distinction between utopian and reformist temporalities breaks down under the conditions of biopolitical production: "Nowadays, each and every reform is radically transformative because we live on an ontological terrain, because our lives are pitched immediately on an ontological level" (Casarino and Negri 2008, 109). As reformist projects with revolutionary aspirations, utopian demands can point in the direction of broader horizons of change, open up new avenues for critical thought and social imagination, and assist in the construction of political subjects who may be better able to think and to want something different. Although the demands for basic income and shorter hours may be proposals for concrete reform rather than systematic transformation, conceiving such demands in relation to their aspirational trajectories and ontological effects confounds facile distinctions between reformist and revolutionary change.

Getting a Life

Certainly these remain risks for a project that poses the antagonism along lines that are at once very broad and also difficult to discern. But as a way to explore further the possibilities of life against work, I want to turn here to a more specific articulation of the rubric that might cast its advantages and disadvantages in a different light. The political project of life against work can also be posed in familiar colloquial terms—in this case, as the mandate to "get a life"[8] As the authors of "The Post-Work Manifesto" declare, "it is time to get a life" (Aronowitz et al. 1998, 40), and in the brief discussion that follows, I want to speculate about how this popular directive might serve to frame a broad and expansive political project.

Let me explain by touching briefly on the three terms of the injunction in reverse order, beginning with the concept of life. The first point to emphasize is that the notion of life referenced in the slogan is not innocent, and it is thus very different from the one deployed in anti-abortion discourse. I mean this in two senses. First, rather than a pure biological life, this life that we would get is nonetheless the object and target of biopower; indeed, the project of life against work is a way to establish the terms of a biopolitical contest, not to recover some lost or imperiled innocence. Second, the life that we might set against work does not pose a simple opposition from a position of exteriority: life is part of work, and work is part of life. Life as an alternative to work does not pretend to be something more authentic and true, which we can find somewhere outside of work. Instead, it must be continually invented in the struggle to mark distinctions between fields of experience that nonetheless remain intertwined.

Neither is it adequately captured by the concept of life more typical of vitalist philosophies, a point that a consideration of the article "a" can illustrate: it is not *the* life that we are encouraged to get, not life as essential common denominator, but a life. It is not for this reason bare life that is invoked, but rather, as James Boggs describes it in the epigraph, "a full life" (1963, 47); it is a life filled with qualities that we are urged toward. This is not to say that it is an individual life. Rather, to draw on Deleuze's description, it is a life of singularities rather than individualities (1997, 4), a life that is common to and shared with others without being the same as theirs.[9] Finally, the injunction is not to get *this* life or *that* life; there is an assumption, by my reading of the phrase, that there will be different lives to get. To borrow another formulation from Deleuze, the indefinite article serves here as "the index of a multiplicity" (5); to say that we should get a life is not to say what its contents might be.

As for the third part of the popular challenge, the activity of "getting" introduces a temporality to the mandate, one that points toward a different future. It is not a call to embrace the life we have, the life that has been made for us—the life of a consumer or a worker, to recall the earlier cautions about what might suffice as a life—but the one that we might want. Deleuze evokes something that may be comparable to this through the distinction between the virtual and the actual: "A life," he explains, "contains only virtuals"; this virtual, however, "is not something that lacks reality, but something that enters into a process of actualization by following the plane that gives it its own reality" (1997, 5). To adapt the insight to my somewhat different purpose here, a life is what each of us needs to get; one cannot get a life if its terms are only dictated from the outside. That said, getting a life is also a necessarily collective endeavor; one cannot get something as big as a life on one's own. And, moreover, though it is a life that would be ours, as a life rather than a commodity, as a web of relations and qualities of experience rather than a possession, it is not something we can be said precisely to own or even to hold. This kind of getting implies a fundamentally different mode of appropriation. The concept of life is not just expansive in this respect, it is also excessive. For Weber, it is the wealth of possibilities that the work ethic diminishes; for Nietzsche, it is what ascetic ideals disavow, but also what can potentially disrupt ascetic modes of containment. A life, by this measure, always exceeds what we have, and its getting is thus necessarily an incomplete process. In short, rather than burdening life with a fixed content—that is, with too many assumptions about what might count as a life beyond work—the possibility of the provocation to get a life lies in its capacity to pose a political project that it does not stipulate and to open a postwork speculative horizon that it cannot fix in advance. My claim is that these commitments to difference, futurity, and excess might render the political project of getting a life less amenable to those forces that would reduce, contain, or appropriate it.

Perhaps more important from the point of view of my argument, the collective effort to get a life can serve as a way both to contest the existing terms of the work society and to struggle to build something new. Seen in this light, the political project of getting a life is both deconstructive and reconstructive, deploying at once negation and affirmation, simultaneously critical and utopian, generating estrangement from the present and provoking a different future. Or, to put it in terms of the concepts around which the book was most broadly organized, it is a project that refuses the existing world of work that is given to us and also demands alternatives.

Notes

1 Cultural representations of the world of work are not only relatively rare but are also often slow to change. Daniel Rodgers gives the example of the continuing use of a cartoon image of a blacksmith to represent workers in the context of an industrial economy in which very few such figures could be found (1978, 242). In the 1960s, James Boggs made a similar point about the problem of clinging to outdated economic imaginaries when he argued that to tell the postindustrial unemployed "that they must work to earn their living is like telling a man in the big city that he should hunt big game for the meat on his table" (1963, 52).

2 Taken together, the two strategies risk replicating the traditional choice between either valuing work or valuing family, in relation to which various "work-family balance" programs remain the most-cited but, it seems to me, singularly in adequatesolution to the conflicts generated by the two spheres' competing claims on our loyalties.

3 Madeline Bunting makes a similar point (2004, 169-70).

4 As Colin Cremin observes, flexible workers are not only expected to achieve employment, but to sustain their fitness for work, their "employability" (2010, 133).

5 Thus, for example, in a book based on interviews with executives at a number of companies that emphasize customer service, the interviewees claim repeatedly that hiring good employees is not about finding people with the right skills, it is about hiring people with the right attitudes (Wiersema 1998).

6 Studies report that across the employment spectrum, attitudes are often more important to managers than aptitude. See, for example, Barnes and Powers (2006,); Beder (2000, 196); Callaghan and Thompson (2002).

7 Talwar reports that the same equation of appearance with professionalism appears in the codes of fast-food management (2002, 100).

8 I explored the injunction to get a life briefly elsewhere in relation to some different concerns (Weeks 2007). I am grateful to the Duke Women's Studies Graduate Scholars Colloquium, and especially Fiona Barnett and Michelle Koerner, for a stimulating discussion of the essay and for helping me to think further about what it might mean to get a life.

9 John Rajchman links Deleuze's concept of life to a conception of society "in which what we have in common is our singularities and not our individualities where what is common is 'impersonal' and what is 'impersonal' is common" (2001, 14).

References

Aronowitz, Stanley, and William DiFazio. 1994. *The Jobless Future: Sci-Tech and the Dogma of Work*. Minneapolis: University of Minnesota Press.

Aronowitz, Stanley, Dawn Esposito, William DiFazio, and Margaret Yard. 1998. "The Post-Work Manifesto." In *Post-Work: The Wages of Cybernation*, edited by Stanley Aronowitz and Jonathan Cutler, 31-80. New York: Routledge.

Barnes, Nora Ganim, and Colleeen E. Powers. 2006. "Beyond the Labor Shortage: Poor Work Ethic and Declining Customer Satisfaction." *Business Forum* 27(2):4-6.

Baudrillard, Jean. 1975. *The Mirror of Production.* Translated by Mark Poster. St Louis: Telos.

Beck, Ulrich. 2000. *The Brave New World of Work.* Translated by Patrick Camiller. Cambridge: Polity.

Beder, Sharon. 2000. *Selling the Work Ethic: From Puritan Pulpit to Corporate PR.* London. Zed. Boggs, James. 1963. *The American Revolution: Pages from a Negro Worker's Notebook.* New York: Monthly Review Press.

Bunting, Madeleine. 2004. *Willing Slaves: How the Overwork Culture is Ruling Our Lives.* London: Harper Collins.

Callaghan, George, and Paul Thompson. 2002. "'We Recruit Attitude': The Selection and Shaping of Routine Call Centre Labour." *Journal of Management Studies* 39 (2): 233-54.

Casarino, Cesare, and Antonio Negri. 2008. *In Praise of the Common: A Conversation on Philosophy and Politics.* Minneapolis: University of Minnesota Press.

Cleaver, Harry. 2000. *Reading* Capital *Politically.* 2nd ed. Leeds, England: Anti/Theses.

Costea, Bogdan, Norman Crump, and Kostas Amiridis. 2008. "Managerialism, the Therapeutic Habitus and the Self in Contemporary Organizing." *Human Relations* 61 (5): 661-85.

Cremin, Colin. 2010. "Never Employable Enough: The (Im)possibility of Satisfying the Boss's Desire." *Organization* 17 (2): 131-49.

Dalla Costa, Mariarosa, and Selma James. 1973. *The Power of Women and the Subversion of the Community.* 2nd ed. Bristol, England: Falling Wall.

Deleuze, Gilles.1988. *Spinoza: Practical Philosophy.* Translated by Robert Hurley. San Francisco: City Light.

——. 1997. "Immanence: A Life…" Translated by Nick Millett. *Theory, Culture, & Society* 14(2): 3-7.

Disch, Lisa J., and Jean M. O'Brien. 2007. "Innovation Is Overtime: An Ethical Analysis of 'Politically Committed' Academic Labor." In *Feminist Waves, Feminist Generations: Life Stories from the Academy,* edited by Hokulani K. Aikau, Karla A. Erickson, and Jennifer L. Pierce, 140-67. Minneapolis: University of Minnesota Press.

Ehrenreich, Barbara. 2001. *Nickel and Dimed: On (Not) Getting By in America.* New York: Henry Holt.

Elson, Diane. 1979. "The Value Theory of Labour." In *Value: The Representation of Labour in Capitalism,* edited by Diane Elson. 115-80. Atlantic Highlands, N.J.: Humanities Press.

Freeman, Carla. 2000. *High Tech and High Heels in the Global Economy: Women, Work, and Pink-Collar Identities in the Caribbean.* Durham: Duke University Press.

Gorz, André. 1999. *Reclaiming Work: Beyond the Wage-Based Society.* Translated by Chris Turner. Cambridge: Polity.

Greenwood, Ernest. 1966. "The Elements of Professionalization." In *Professionalization,* edited by Howard M. Vollmer and Donald L. Mills, 9-19. Englewood Cliffs, N.J.: Prentice-Hall.

Hardt, Michael, and Antonio Negri. 2000. *Empire.* Cambridge: Harvard University Press.

Henwood, Doug. 1997. "Talking about Work." *Monthly Review* 49 (3): 18-30.

Hochschild, Arlie. 1983. *The Managed Heart: The Commercialization of Human Feeling.* Berkeley: University of California Press.

Kolakowski, Leszek. 1978. *Main Currents of Marxism: Its Rise, Growth, and Dissolution.* Vol. 2. Translated by P.S. Falla. Oxford: Clarendon Press of Oxford University Press.

Lafargue, Paul. 1898. *The Right to Be Lazy: Being a Refutation of the "Right to Work" of 1848.* Translated by Harriet E. Lothrop. New York: International Publishing.

Leidner, Robin. 1996, "Rethinking Questions of Control: Lessons from McDonald's." In *Working in the Service Society*, edited by Cameron Lynne Macdonald and Carmen Sirianni, 29-49. Philadelphia: Temple University Press.

Mill, John Stuart. 1988. *The Subjection of Women.* Indianapolis: Hackett.

Mills, C. Wright. 1951. *White Collar: The American Middle Classes.* New York: Oxford University Press.

Morris, William. 1999. "Useful Work Versus Useless Toil." In William Morris, *William Morris on Art and Socialism*, edited by Norman Kelvin, 128-43. Mineola, N.Y.: Dover.

Negri, Antonio. 1991. *Marx Beyond Marx: Lessons on the Grundisse.* Translated by Harry Cleaver, Michael Ryan, and Maurizio Viano. Brooklyn, N.Y.: Autonomedia.

——.2005. *Books for Burning: Between Civil War and Democracy in 1970s Italy.* Translated by Timothy S. Murphy, Arianna Bove, Ed Emory, and Francesca Novella. New York: Verso.

Peters, Tom. 1997. "The Brand Called You." *Fast Company* 10: 83-94.

Peterson, Spike V. 2003. *A Critical Rewriting of Global Political Economy: Integrating Reproductive, Productive, and Virtual Economies.* New York: Routledge.

Postone, Moishe. 1996. *Time, Labor, and Social Domination: A Reinterpretation of Marx's Critical Theory.* Cambridge: Cambridge University Press.

Rajchman, John. 2001. Introduction. In Gilles Deleuze, *Pure Immanence: Essays on A Life*, translated by Anne Boyman, 7-23. New York: Zone.

Rodgers, Daniel T. 1978. *The Work Ethic in Industrial America: 1850-1920.* Chicago: University of Chicago Press.

Ross, Andrew. 2003. *No-Collar: The Humane Workplace and Its Hidden Costs.* New York: Basic.

Talwar, Jennifer Parker. 2002. *Fast Food, Fast Track: Immigrants, Big Business, and the American Dream.* Boulder, Colo.: Westview.

Townley, Barbara. 1989. "Selection and Appraisal: Reconstituting 'Social Relations'?" In *New Perspectives on Human Resource Management*, edited by John Storey, 92-108. London: Routledge.

Vercellone, Carlo. 1996. "The Anomaly and
Exemplariness of the Italian Welfare State."
Translated by Michael Hardt. In *Radical
Thought in Italy: A Potential Politics*, edited by
Paolo Virno and Michael Hardt, 81-96.
Minneapolis: University of Minnesota Press.

Virno, Paolo. 1996. "Virtuosity and Revolution:
The Political Theory of Exodus." Translated by
Ed Emory. In *Radical Thought in Italy: A
Potential Politics,* edited by Paolo Virno and
Michael Hardt, 189-210. Minneapolis:
University of Minnesota Press.

——. 2004. *A Grammar of the Multitude.*
Translated by Isabella Bertoletti, James
Cascaito, and Andrea Casson. Los Angeles:
Semiotext(e).

Weber, Max. 1946. "Science as a Vocation."
In Max Weber, From *Max Weber: Essays in
Sociology*, translated and edited by H.H. Gerth
and C. Wright Mills, 129-56. New York: Oxford
University Press.

Weeks, Kathi. 2007. "Life within and against
Work: Affective Labor, Feminist Critique, and
Post-Fordist Politics." *Ephemera* 7 (1): 233-49.

Wiersema, Fred. Ed. 1998. *Customer Service:
Extraordinary Results at Southwest Airlines,
Charles Schwab, Lands' End, American
Express, Staples and USAA*. New York:
Harper Business.w

'MAINLINING' LIFE INTO DEAD LABOR

Carl Cederström and Peter Fleming

The screwball characters of the child/adult's television programme *The Muppet Show* might seem far from the stupefying atmosphere of the modern corporation. But capitalism has become strange. While work is still something we would rather avoid like the plague, the tyrannical boss has been replaced by another figure: the passive aggressive Human Resource Manager. Armed with the latest kitchen-sink psychology, and behaving like David Brent from *The Office,* convinced that his real talents lie in performance art, this new architect of corporate culture attempts to convince workers that they should enjoy their own exploitation. Their aim is clear. Not only to make us do something we would rather shun, but also make us *want to do it.*

Picture the scene: On a chilly Monday morning a group of twelve call center workers feel a twinge of anxiety as they leave their 'call-pods' and file into a large meeting room. The firm—let us call it 'Sunray Customer Service'—are well informed about the alienating nature of labor, especially when it comes to the mind numbing, depressing and frequently humiliating job of a call center slave. But Sunray management had a clever idea.

Knowing that it was only when its workers had checked-out (either literally or mentally) that they begin to feel human again and buzz with life; knowing, also, that call center work requires high levels of social intelligence, innovation and emotional initiative; knowing all these things, Sunray had to find a way of capturing and replicating that buzz of life...on the job.

Capitalism has always destroyed the thing it needs the most. But when it is the very humanity of the employee—his or her capacity to communicate, think creatively and be social—an array of hired occupational scientists have attempted the impossible: to *inject life into the dead-zone of work*. Managers at Sunray were rabid enthusiasts of this human technology. It encouraged employees to treat the call center as if it was their home or a late night party. As the training manuals and motivation talks relentlessly reminded them:

> Most call centers treat their employees like battery hens. Not Sunray. We are free rangers and respect that everyone is different and special.

The mantra repeated in an Orwell-meets-Oprah manner was 'Just be yourself!' All of those elements of personality that were once barred from work—sexuality, lifestyle, fashion tastes, obsessions with pop stars and health food—have now become welcome, if not demanded, on the job. If you are gay, that's great! If you hate capitalism, wonderful! If you are of Nepalese ethnic descent, perfect! For there is no better call center worker than one who can improvise around the script, breathe life into a dead role and pretend their living death is in fact the apogee of life.

Back to the Sunray meeting-room on that cool Monday morning. The workers looked at the floor anxiously, feigning smiles but knowing that something pretty awful was about to happen. They were told to form a circle as Carla—the 'team development leader' —prepared to deliver a pep-talk, which would have been funny if not for the sadistic glint in her eye. 'As you all know, life at Sunray is more than just a job, it's all about fun and enjoying yourself, here you can really shine and be yourself!' The workers shifted nervously as she bleated on, 'And it's all about color and fun...OK guys, lets do it!.' 'Oh Jesus' muttered one worker with blue hair and an anarchist tattoo on his wrist. Carla hit PLAY on her out-dated CD player and we all began to sing Kermit the Frog's only Top-10 single: *Why are there, so many, songs about rainbows, what*

makes the world go round...someday we'll find it, the rainbow
connection, the lovers, the dreamers and me ...

This team building exercise, which one of the authors observed
when studying new methods of exploitation in the service sector,
seems remote from the large-scale power shifts reshaping a waning
late-capitalism. However, we suggest that it is indicative of how
novel forms of regulation are focusing on those moments of life that
once flourished beyond the remit of the corporation. Like a desperate junkie that resorts to 'mainlining' (injecting straight into the
vein) to sustain an unsustainable condition, moribund-style capitalism is attempting to revive its flagging fortunes by turning to
that which it has always killed...living labor. We know from Marx's
prophetic study of capital that living labor is its central source of
value. This is defined primarily by movement and sociality, our
creation of a common world—*our* world—that is rich with recipro-
cal social relations, networks of co-operation and mutual aid. *This
is the ironic communist underbelly of capitalism.* On the outside,
capital may seem fluid, dynamic and full of creative possibilities,
but that is part of its mythology. In fact the opposite is evident once
we free our selves from the mentality of work. Marx is clear on this
point. What to us appears to be a creative movement—the essence
of life itself—is in fact a cunning ruse fabricated by the frenetic
and goal orientated nature of *speed-labor.* Despite all the hustle,
nothing really changes. Only when the sleeper awakes and soberly
considers life from the position of non-work does the figure of the
dead man working come into sharp relief. Perhaps what is different
today, however, is the crucial ideological function that the fantasy
of "non-work" plays. Ironically, imagining ourselves elsewhere only
binds us tighter to that which we seek to escape.

The corporation's turn to those living moments that persist beyond
the dead lands of economic rationality indicates a major shift in
the nature of power at work today. Sunray's idiotic evocation of
The Muppets is a far cry from how work used to be organized. The
proto-typical factory supervisor or office manager considered play,
humour, sexuality and personal idiosyncrasies an impediment to

the rational pursuit of productivity. The 'human factor' still existed of course, flourishing beneath the radar in informal games and sub-cultures, but management viewed this as a dangerous underworld of autonomy. Something to be eradicated. Consider the 1960s factory depicted in Huw Beynon's classic *Working for Ford* (where workers were admonished with the motto: 'when we are at work, we work, when that is done only then can we play'). Or consider Max Weber's dark description of the bureaucratic office and its systematic annihilation of love, passion and individuality. All of this is a universe away from working at Sunray. Even the 1980s IBM-led 'corporate culture' craze, which modelled the enterprise after the family, maintained a sharp line between work and non-work. This separation was observed by Gideon Kunda in his famous study, *Engineering Culture,* where he recalls one employee chastising a co-worker who had confessed that overwork had driven him to alcoholism: 'you keep that kind of shit to yourself.' At Sunray, however, anything and everything personal—warts and all—was welcome. Why this sea change in managerial thought and the rules of exploitation?

The reason is two-fold. Firstly, it relates to a crisis of capital that compels it to search for a spark of life at work in increasingly desperate ways. Secondly, the *virus of being at work* has spread throughout the social body, seeking more and more uncommercial moments to make money from. A good starting point to unravel this transformation is the *crisis* of Fordism. From the 1970s and into the 1980s Western capitalism was rocked by a number of crises that were internal (debt and stagnation) and external (the oil embargo). It could no longer organize itself and generate the rate of profit required. Two important developments followed. First, the deindustrialization of the West and the concomitant growth of service work; second, and more importantly for us, the displacement of the management function onto labor itself. Indeed, capital realized it could no longer organize itself; thus, better to enlist the workforce to carry out the job themselves. This massive dependency on labor could have hastened the end of work and the sweet abolition of capital forever. But it didn't.

One only has to turn to academic work to see how this involves a substantial change in power relations whereby work becomes a continuous *way of life,* rather than just something we do among other things. The academic today dutifully writes his lectures on a Sunday night, explores new ideas while half asleep, arrives at class punctually, trains himself in the art of writing, reading, and communicating. As a result the corporatized university makes grotesque surpluses out of a self-fashioned craft (and, yes, it is sadly ironic that one of the authors is writing this sentence on a very sunny Easter Friday). This typifies how hierarchies of regulation have been *horizontalized.* Most of us still have a boss above us giving orders. But we have also partially internalized this 'boss function.' Whereas under Fordism workers could mentally tell the boss to 'fuck off' as they left the factory, now they take it home with them. Turning-off is no longer an available option. Might not this be capitalism's ultimate Frankensteinian moment? (Recall the curse Frankenstein received from his jilted monster: *I shall be with you on your wedding night!*)

This might be one reading of Gilles Deleuze's classic essay 'Postscript on the Societies of Control.' Whereas Foucault argued that the template of the prison had permeated all of society including the factory, Deleuze surmised he had got it the wrong way around. It was the factory—not an actual factory, but the factory in its *virtual form,* as a way of life, a gaseous ethos—that has infected our biosphere. When we breathe the molecules of the social foundry, we always 'owe the man,' are indebted to the boss, the master. The sheer totality of this state of affairs is what makes Deleuze paranoid:

> In a society of control, the corporation has replaced the factory, and the corporation is a spirit, a gas...In the disciplinary societies one was always starting again (from school to the barracks, from the barracks to the factory), while in the societies of control one is never finished with anything—the corporation, the educational system, the armed services being metastable states coexisting in

one and the same modulation, like a universal system
of deformation.

The traditional line-in-the-sand between capital and labor no
longer makes sense to anyone. Today, the real struggle is between
capital and *life* (bios), although the struggle is not played out under
especially fair rules, given that we can hardly tell what life is any-
more. We should consider here what Foucault and his followers
have called *bio-power*. If work was once primarily regulated by
bureaucracy through depersonalization then today we witness the
emergence of a new regime of control which we call *biocracy*, in
which life itself is an essential 'human resource' to be exploited.

Perhaps this is why we find our sentimental friend, Kermit the Frog,
entering the call center as a vehicle for tapping into the life force of
labor. This is not an isolated case. Life itself is now the most lucra-
tive kind of capital being put to work, from the hipstermarketing
firm to the call center sweatshop. Work is now presented as the
Siamese twin to life, as the sphere in which life can most fully
thrive. Personal preferences of the employee of the month—choice
of music, favourite food, and historical heroes—are presented on a
monitor in the office's foyer. And workers are encouraged to bring
personal items to work. Pictures of beloved children and dogs, a
banner of the favourite football team and souvenirs bought from
that distant holiday in Lanzarote are intermingled with piles of
paper in the cubicle. Moreover, popmanagement books abound on
the topic of play, fun and authenticity with the hope of rendering
work into a paradoxical moment of non-work. In his best seller, *The
Seven Day Weekend,* management guru Ricardo Semler argues that
work and life are now one. The blurb on the back cover is telling:

> Imagine a company where employees set their own hours;
> where there are no offices, no job titles, no business plans;
> where employees get to endorse or veto any new venture;
> where kids are encouraged to run the halls; and where the
> CEO lets other people make nearly all the decisions…if you
> have the freedom to get your job done on your own terms and

to blend your work life and personal life with enthusiasm and creative energy. Smart bosses will eventually realize that you might be most productive if you work on Sunday afternoon, play golf on Monday morning, go to a movie on Tuesday afternoon, and watch your child play soccer on Thursday.

It is easy to see why some workers lament the good old days when at least they could leave their kids at home rather than be hounded by them at the office as well! But does this mean that work and life might now be somehow reconciled, that a 'frictionless capitalism' has finally arrived? No. This trend is pure ideology since it seeks to intensify our unfreedom in the language of non-work. Yet work remains in its Deleuzian 'gaseous' form, which is the exact opposite of play, fun, and real living. Therefore, the latter needs to be staged, manufactured, scripted and ultimately *imitated* in the office. As the Sunray call center example indicates, the obvious weakness of this manufactured and faux life resides in its coercive nature. Employees have little choice but to participate in yet another humiliating teambuilding exercise. If asked to wear their pyjamas to work (on the much dreaded 'pyjama day') or sing a silly Muppets song, they had better not object. Being a party-pooper is today the most serious crime you could commit, even worse than taking these exercises to the extreme (wearing an indecently provocative pyjama, or singing in the exact, unbearably loud and shrill, voice of the Muppets). Herein lies a curious aspect of *biocracy,* what we might call a *formalized informality.* You are forced, weirdly, to be yourself. And what other response could be made to this ridiculous demand than the one already made by our anarchist worker, when he forlornly mumbled 'Oh, Jesus...?' (And no, he was not consider-ing this a serious cry for help; he was a committed atheist).

Extending workplace regulation by imitating life serves an important economic role when capitalism becomes super-reliant on human qualities like social intelligence, reciprocity, communica-tion and shared initiative. These aspects of being human often lie outside or beyond the logic of economic rationality, as Paulo Virno succinctly puts it:

The productive cooperation in which labor-power participates is always larger and richer than the one put into play by the labor process. It includes also the world of non-labor, the experiences and knowledge matured outside of the factory and the office. Labor-power increases the value of capital only because it never loses its qualities of non-labor.

This places the corporation in a precarious position. After all, it is only that which is non-exploited, non-controlled and freely expressed which can provide the raw material for 'cognitive capitalism' today—a basic requirement of even the most menial work, as our call center example reveals. Indeed, social intelligence often develops *despite* the regulations of the typical workplace, not because of them. Peter Blau observed this in his classic study of office politics in the 1960s. In an attempt to convey their discontent, employees did something strange: *exactly what they were told to do, following the formal rules to the letter.* As a result, when the invisible wealth of informal engagement, knowledge sharing, and mutual aid was withdrawn, the office was brought to a halt. The implications of Blau's study is clear: the formal corporate form actually *obstructs* the creation of wealth, and is thus completely reliant on an undercurrent of non-commercialized living labor, the very thing it cannot help but demolish as soon as it gets its anxious hands on it.

It is now fairly obvious what was happening at the Sunray call center. Here, the demand to 'just be yourself' was nothing but a cunning way of capturing the much needed sociality of the employee: affability on the phone, friendliness, and intuition—all of which are crucial in interactive customer service work. Importantly, this transforms our vision of the corporation from something that *creates* value to something that encloses it. As Lazzarato argues, 'the enterprise does not create its object (goods) but *the world within which the object exists*...the enterprise does not create its subjects (workers and consumers) but *the world within which the subject exists.*' For us, however, Lazzarato seems to be ceding too much credit to the corporation.

As Marx's thesis on dead labor implies, capital can't even create these two worlds, since only living entities can make a world, a home, a space and time of co-existence.

Finally, this displacement of non-work into the office also entails the obverse, the shift of work into all pockets of life. As we have already demonstrated, our so-called worker's society is a hermeneutically sealed totality in which *we are always at work.* And therefore always entangled in a moment of living death. The traditional point of production—say the factory assembly line—is scattered to every corner of our lives since it is our very sociality that creates value for business. As Andrew Ross noted in his study of the IT firm Razorfish, 'ideas and creativity were just as likely to surface at home or in other locations, and so employees were encouraged to work elsewhere…the goal was to extract value from every waking moment of an employee's day.'

But it is not only when this new bio-political proletariat is awake that they are working. Value is being created even in their most intimate and vulnerable states, when asleep. This is vividly captured in a recent biographical essay by Rob Lucas, 'Dreaming in Code.' The computer programmer described how his life was so integrated with his job that sleep was even involved, dreaming up solutions to complex code conundrums (what he called 'sleep working') in the middle of the night. He writes, 'dreaming about your work is one thing, but dreaming inside the logic of your work is another…in the kind of dream I have been having the very movement of my mind is transformed: it has become that of my job.' Such sleep working was not experienced as an amplification of life. On the contrary, it represented a subtraction, a vampire-like negation of his vital existence for the benefit of an impersonal and repellent institutional imposition. A job.

* * *

As exploitation is generalized in time and space like an invisible gas, an absolute worker's society emerges, a society in which neither life nor death appears on the horizon. We know this place. We know the smell and taste of the perpetual living death in the office, on the commuter bus, in the dark mine, or the restroom of an empty office tower in the middle of the night—even in our dreams.

British language style has been preserved in this reprinted essay.

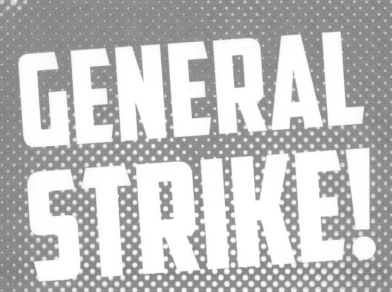

GENERAL STRIKE!

AY 1ST

NO WORK, NO SCHOOL, NO HOUSEWORK, NO SHOPPING, NO BANKING...

DISCOVER THE POWER OF REFUSAL!

DEBT

WE ARE YOUR NEIGHBORS | WE ARE YOUR FAMILY | WE ARE YOUR FRIENDS

JOIN THE RESISTANCE

WE ARE THE 99% • OCCUPY WALL STREET • BRING YOUR FRIENDS
FINANCIAL DISTRICT • S17NYC.ORG • SEPT 15-17 2012 • STRIKEDEBT.ORG

AFTER WORK: WHAT DOES REFUSAL MEAN TODAY?

Peter Fleming

3:06 a.m., silent, dark. My bed felt like a prison. Sleep should be the opposite, an escape. But something happened at the office and was now bothering me more and more. In the future, of course, I'll look back and see it for what it really is: a trivial and petty thing. Certainly unworthy of the existential energy being sapped from me. But at 3:06 a.m., things look very different. My job becomes everything, feeling more like a virus infecting my body rather than something I merely do among other things. As a result, all perspective is lost.

This anecdote, which most of us can relate to, captures how neoliberalism enlists us to perform its labor today. My job, body, worries and sense of self are knotted into a singular moment without conclusion. How did we reach this point where we see no end or "outside" to this otherwise insignificant activity we call work? And how on earth do we resist it?

To begin with, some historical shifts in capitalism are important to note. Under earlier Fordist systems of production, the time and place of our work was very clear. Within these parameters we fought a pitched battle over its quality, amount, and autonomy. Most jobs were undoubtedly boring and exploitative, but we were able to marginally separate it from the rest of our lives by checking out.

With the crisis of Fordism in Western economies it quickly become evident that capitalism was seriously unable to organize itself. As a result, a reconfiguration took place to save it. The management function was displaced onto workers themselves. This did not do away with supervisors above us giving orders. But it did give rise to auxiliary modes of power like self-managing teams, the portfolio career, hyper-individualized work practices, flexi-employment, and discretionary emotional labor. Suddenly 'life itself' is drawn into the work process.

This certainly represents a quantitative shift in capitalist regulation—more time spent in the office or worrying about it. But it is, more importantly, a *qualitative* change, too. Our jobs now become something very intimate to us, especially when it relies upon our social aptitudes, creative energies, and emotional intelligence to make things happen—as many occupations do today. And when the logic of production is embedded in our very social being it is difficult to check out. Its power comes not only from above—a supervisor or deadline—but also from the side and below. We begin to live with our work and it with us. And this pressure is certainly exacerbated in today's climate when the only thing that worries us more than our jobs is the thought of not having one.

In this broader context of self-administration/self-policing, it is important to note two aspects of neoliberalism's relationship to work if we are to successfully resist it. Firstly, by transforming employees into abstract "human resources" and "human capital," the objective necessity of work is blended with our personal sense of individuality and social intellect. Again, much of this is the result of the jobs we do today in the West (so-called immaterial labor). But an equally important driver is late capitalism's inability to organize itself through conventional command and control structures. Crisis is central here. As a result, it now needs us to be constantly concerned with its problems, integrating them into our "life problems" in order to get things done. This is basically how bio-power functions. Work and life itself become indistinguishable …or so we think.

Secondly, resisting work and employment is now tricky because what exactly do we target? Ourselves? This difficulty is no accident. It is specifically how neoliberalism aims to eliminate effective opposition. When our jobs are overly embodied, attached to us both inside and outside the office, working is essentially an *ideological* practice rather than something required by objective necessity (e.g., paying the bills). Unlike other ideologies, however, it does not function by convincing us how wonderful and brilliant it is. Even its most right-wing advocates no longer believe this. Instead, it seeks to universalize the very template of work so that we cannot discern any outside reference point or horizon. For better or worse, we are stuck with it forever.

This is why many people experience their jobs today as an endless way of life. Yes, deeply unpleasant and meaningless, but also something we can never be finished with or forget. Like a debt that can never be repaid, the weight of work feels inescapable. It is with this illusion that neoliberalism most successfully entraps us.

The book I wrote with Carl Cederström, *Dead Man Working,* attempts to demonstrate this point in a rather morbid discussion about job-related suicides occurring throughout the West. While undoubtedly tragic and exceptional, we thought this trend said something more generally about the integration of work and life today. From the outside, the thought of killing yourself over a dull little thing like work is unfathomable. Over a lost lover, yes. Ennui? Perhaps. But a stupid little office job or even worse, a bank's bullying letters about the mortgage? Never. Just quit. Walk away. Sadly, however, like our troubled sleeper at 3:06 a.m., the suicidal clerk has no perspective. The fetish of work poisons everything. Only then does a violent end seem like the only way out. Life and labor are perfectly blended. And is this not neoliberal capitalism's highest ideal?

Given this state of affairs, we are, in fact, much better placed to approach the idea of refusing work. Three points are significant. First, the real reason we work so much today (or are obsessed with it if we are now part of the growing reserve army of the unemployed) has very little to do with survival. Sure, the bills need to be paid, etc. But the broader ritual of working is now fairly detached from economic necessity. It is imposed for its own sake. As a result, we cannot say to ourselves, "we have done enough," since like all rituals, it functions by way of a self-referential loop. The UK Conservative government's controversial Back-to-Work scheme illustrates this perfectly. The unemployed are forced to sweat in fast-food restaurants without pay. The message is clear: this has nothing to do with material self-preservation; it is more about maintaining an ideological habit or addiction and the lack of perspective this engenders. This conceptual move is the first step refusing work today. It must not be confused with refusing oneself or economic necessity (i.e., survival). Indeed, the contrary.

This is not to say that there are not large groups of people whose work is directly linked to material subsistence, especially in the Global South and among the working poor in the North. The ideology of work I am referring to concerns the way in which almost every activity in Western societies appears to be linked to this sign of necessity i.e., work which has now ballooned into an all encompassing template for life itself. It must be remembered that before the arrival of capitalism, the average time spent "working" was about three days a week. Someone from another period would look at us and think we were crazy. Rubbing salt into the wound is that despite all of this work we are still precarious, poor, anxious, worried, struggling.

Related to this, we should also be vigilant about the way the global ultra-poor is used by neoliberal apologists to justify the Western obsession with work. Someone might say to us, for example, "hey, you think you've got it bad, just look at the sewer worker in Soweto...you can't complain." A nice double bind is thereby created. Accept your relatively well-off, overworked miserable life, because the only alternative is being knee-deep in effluent in a Third World sewer. Well, perhaps neither option is acceptable.

This is not enough, of course, which brings us to the second point. Merely realizing that work is made-up does not make being evicted any less real when you fail to pay the rent. So we need to dig deeper into the causes of this strange over-ritualization of labor and identify what it does to us individually and collectively. It is the depressing feeling of endlessness that really defines the condition of working today, mainly because we are always carrying it with us, recognizing it in our gait and dreams of a future that only reflects itself.

This fantasy of permanence is one of neoliberalism's crowning achievements. So it ought to be our next target, ejecting it from our bodies and relations with others. We have known for quite a while that capitalism exploits us primarily through *time*. Time at work. Time thinking about work. Time preparing for work. What makes neoliberalism so much more transgressive than earlier modes of capitalist control lies in the way it universalizes the temporal register of work, erasing any sense of end or beginning. We are always checked in, but never quite know when or how.

In light of this, perhaps resisting work not only means refusing the concrete time it steals from us, but also disrupting the fantasy of its never-ending ubiquity. That this is frequently done in self-destructive ways is understandable. But a more sustainable strategy aims to establish inoperative thresholds—that is, collective forms of life that are no more productive than they need to be. The line is arbitrary no doubt, and this is what makes it so powerful. We can bring the level to zero. Moreover, surplus or superfluous productiveness can only be identified through social "endpoints," ones that, for want of a better term, have been incredibly *de-worked*. The idea does not mean that nothing gets done, in fact the opposite. Social labor is freed from the deadening strictures of economic instrumentality that we currently call work so that purposeful activity can be pursued once again. This can be seen in jobs that we might identify with and take pleasure in. It is the wonders of living labor we are enjoying rather than work, since its qualities are based upon open self-determination rather than structured exploitation.

None of this has anything to do with "work-life" balance programs, which have always been a scam to reconcile us to our own exploitation. Nor is it related to idleness, laziness, or even illness, all of which have been considered in the post-workerist literature. The problem with these practices is they tend to reinforce the broader backdrop of a work-saturated society. If Gilles Deleuze was correct to suggest that any dominant form of power functions through "pinching time" and reverberating its specific qualities throughout life as such, then any proper reclamation of social time requires a new political pinch.

The problem with capitalist work relations today is not about having too little time away from our jobs. Contemporary cognitive capitalism requires that we have plenty of that. Some take holidays (if they are lucky), weekends, and so-forth. Neoliberalism does not function by taking over these non-work zones. It would not survive if it did, as I shall demonstrate below. All it needs to do is *index* them to the ideology of work.

I recently spoke with a tired, overworked middle manager who illustrates how this functions. His company forced him to take a vacation after four years of non-stop work. Along with his partner, a two-week holiday in Crete looked like wonderful opportunity to relax. Three days in he soon realized something was very wrong. He desperately needed a fix. Telling his partner that the previous evening's meal disagreed with him, he retreated to the bathroom with a smuggled Blackberry to clear work emails.

The case tells us much. Last summer the *New York Times* even ran an article called "How to Have a Vacation." Its readers not only have little idea what to do with their free time, but actually view it as some kind of black hole. Like a smoker who has decided to quit the habit, the temporal register of non-working is experienced as a vapid emptiness.

What appears to be a symptom of its power is in fact a weak link in the ideology of work. It is how we experience or "pinch" our free or non-work time that is critical. Once we get that right, then it is just a matter of escalating and amplifying it into something new. But what?

As we demonstrated in *Dead Man Working*, so many attempts to induce a limit or "afterwards" to working life today end up becoming individualistic moments of escape. Passing out from too much alcohol. Burnout. Suicide. Even yoga. However understandable, these practices do make the major mistake of accepting the bio-political ideal that life and work are the same. Escaping work is thus a matter of escaping life itself. So we must break this spell by insisting that work has nothing to do with life. Refusing work is a matter of exiting *into* life, reclaiming it back ourselves, that is to say, to live again. But what exactly is a livable life? It depends of course. But it might be defined as a way of living that does not pray for its own end, does not proceed with the precept that any kind of conclusion or terminus would be infinitely preferable. And where might we find this "livable life"? Ironically, perhaps, everywhere. Is this not the open secret of neoliberal capitalism? Because of its inherently antisocial tenets, it cannot reproduce itself on its own terms. That is to say, if we had pure and unadulterated free markets, commercialization, private ownership, and individualism, society would implode under its own weight. Neoliberalism persists *despite* itself, relying upon a vast amount of non-commercial and highly socialized labor to carry on. People making do; forging a "livable life" between shifts and hangovers; artisanal amateurism and spontaneous cooperation. And much of this labor is antithetical to the principles of corporatization because it involves mutual aid, open access, free work, counterplanning, and so forth. How else would a city like London, for example, survive given the immense disparity between wages and the cost of living? What is being exploited is everything the present system cannot provide on its own accord. The perversity of neoliberal capitalism lies here since it does not actually work.

The underlying presence of this non-productive labor can be observed in individual workplaces, too. More seasoned management consultants call it the all important "good will factor." It is a social reservoir that makes things happen, even if it remains unacknowledged or unremunerated. We see it most evidently when it is withdrawn. For example, if everyone simply followed the rules of neo-managerialism to the letter, almost nothing would get done. Most organizations require a massive amount of "invisible labor" inside and outside its formal domain to function. This strange unworkable aspect of capitalist rationality was a central point we wanted to convey in *Dead Man Working*.

Now we have arrived at the nub of the problem concerning the refusal of work and the possibility of a post-work future. Working today is not only mythological (rather than bound by economic necessity) but also extremely *parasitical*. It rides upon our collective efforts to make a livable life together, transforming those shared energies into an unbearable situation once again. Here is the political question: can this collective threshold of non-productiveness (or what some have called the "under common") be reclaimed towards more civilized ends? Or is it destined to remain what David Harvey labeled a "negative common," forever serving a parasitical capitalist system?

I remain optimistic. We can already see the beginnings of a radical repossession movement among the growing disenfranchised working classes (which now includes almost everybody). The common is being retained. From the co-operatives in Southern Europe to the *fabricas recuperadas* ("recovered factories") trend in Argentina in which deserted zones of production are reclaimed by the unemployed, self-valorization and detachment are central concepts for understanding what time looks like after work. Most importantly, these post-work worlds are not in some far away, inscrutable future. Once we appreciate that it is in fact the living material that a semi-dead neoliberalism depends upon to persist, another world appears before us—rich, enjoyable, and authentically endless.

In conclusion, Bonnie Ware, a nurse who cares for terminally ill patients, recently reported on the most common regrets they expressed when close to death. First and foremost was not being true to themselves, living a life that had little to do with what they really wanted. And second, they simply wished they had not worked so much. All of that time, effort, and worry seemed like such a waste. For them it was too late. But what about for us? If only we could embody that final realization throughout our entire lives, workplaces, neighborhoods, homes, unconscious desires...

Image Credits

7–8
School Is a Factory, 1978/80,
Allan Sekula, exhibition copy 2011,
gray scale pigment prints. Courtesy
of the artist and gallery Michel Rein,
Paris.

45–46
Unemployment Office (Arbeids-
formidlingens lokaler), 1978, Oslo.
Clients are still greeted individually
and data systems are not yet in use.
© Arbeiderbladet (the workers
magazine). Courtesy of the Labor
Movement Archives and Library
of Oslo.

59–60
International Women's Day
demonstration, March 8, 1975, Oslo.
© Courtesy of the Labor Movement
Archives and Library of Oslo.

79–80
Albertine, sculpture by
Alfred Seland, City Hall, Oslo.
© Photo: Brent G. Betz.

89
National Union of Women Workers,
Copenhagen Central division's
demonstration for equal pay
(storkøbenhavnske afdelingers
demonstration for ligeløn), March 2,
1973. Photo: unknown.
© The Workers' Museum & The Labor
Movement's Library and Archives,
Denmark.

90
Wildana tøffelfabrikk (slipper
factory) in Halden, Oslo, 1971.
Photo: unknown © Arbeiderbladet,
Courtesy of the Labor Movement
Archives and Library of Oslo.

91
Volvo factory in Torslanda, Sweden,
1964. Photo: unknown © the Labor
Movement Archives and Library
of Oslo.

92
National Union of Women Workers
take iniative to decorate buses in
Copenhagen with demands for equal
pay. Photo: Ernst Nielsen, 1973.
Printed with permission from his
widow. © The Workers' Museum
& The Labor Movement's Library
and Archives, Denmark.

93
The Union's March 8 in Folkets Hus
(The People's House), Enghavevej,
Copenhagen, 1987. © Photo:
Ole Wildt. The Workers' Museum
& The Labor Movement's Library and
Archives, Denmark.

94
Intl. Women's Day, Oslo, 1977. Photo: unknown © the Labor Movement Archives and Library of Oslo.

Redstockings (Rødstrømpernes), Fælledpark happening, also included the capturing and honoring of the man of the day, Copenhagen, 1970. © Photo: Jørgen Schiøttz. Printed with permission from Inge Balling. Courtesy of Arbejdermuseet & Arbejderbevægelsens Bibliotek og Arkiv/The Workers' Museum & The Labor Movement's Library and Archives.

95
Redstockings, famous bus action, getting on bus line 21 and refusing to pay more than 80% of the ticket, equivalent to womens' salaries, Copenhagen 1970. Photographer: Jørgen Schiøttz. © Printed with permission from Inge Balling. Arbejdermuseet & Arbejderbevægelsens Bibliotek og Arkiv/ The Workers' Museum & The Labor Movement's Library and Archives.

Equal pay demonstration, Copenhagen, February 8, 1971. © Photo: Ernst Nielsen. Reprinted with permission from Birgit Gudrun. The Workers' Museum & The Labor Movement's Library and Archives, Denmark.

96
Womens Day, March 8, 1976. From 'Samarbeidsutvalgets tog,' Oslo. Photo: unknown. © the Labor Movement Archives and Library of Oslo.

National Union of Women Workers, Section 4 – Iron Women, *Kvindeligt Arbejderforbund afd. 4 – jernets kvinder* had their own demonstration. From Rosenørns Allé to Vester Voldgade, Copenhagen they demonstrated for union demands, with emphasis on equal pay, 1969. © The Workers' Museum & The Labor Movement's Library and Archives, Denmark.

97–98
School is A Factory, 1978/80, Allan Sekula, exhibition copy 2011, gray scale pigment prints. Courtesy of the artist and gallery Michel Rein, Paris.

127–128
Rikshospitalet (National Hospital), Oslo, January 1980. Workers taking lunch. In the background tools are being sterilized in the autoclave. Photo: Joanna Butler © the Labor Movement Archives and Library of Oslo.

177–178
Drawing from the pictorial novel *Soft City*, 1969–75, Pushwagner, ink on paper 41.8 × 29.8 cm. © Pushwagner/BONO 2013.

189
May Day, poster, New York, 2012.
© Design: Josh MacPhee,
Brooklyn, NY.

190
Join the Resistance, by R Black, 2012.
First appeared in Tidal magazine,
issue #3. Courtesy of artist and MTL.

Arbeidstid images
Installation views, all courtesy of
Henie Onstad Kunstsenter (HOK).

Photographers
Ibghy & Lemmens
34–35

Camilla Sune
20–21; 27; 32–33; 33; 40^2; 41; 52

Øystein Thorvaldsen
26; 28–29; 31; 36–37; 40^1; 42–43

ARBEIDSTID

Henie Onstad Kunstsenter (HOK), Oslo

May 23–September 1, 2013

Artists

Jesper Alvær

Duncan Campbell

Marianne Flotron

Paul Graham

Tehching Hsieh

Richard Ibghy & Marilou Lemmens

Kleines Postfordistisches Drama

Sharon Lockhart

MTL {Nitasha Dhillon & Amin Husain}

Michala Paludan

Olivia Plender

Allan Sekula & Noël Burch

Artists Presentations

Jesper Alvær

b. 1973, Copenhagen, Denmark
lives and work in Oslo.

I received my formal education at
the University of Oslo and at the
Academy of Fine Arts in Prague.
Several of my recent projects share a
fascination for work and employment
processes as something difficult to
grasp and distinguish as such. My
installation for the exhibition
"Arbeidstid" is a film based on
experiences and material generated
during the first four months of 2011
in Oslo. During this period I system-
atically organized forty-two meet-
ings with people I employed for the
day. During that day we discussed
the nature and premises for this
particular employment situation and
our time spent together as a job. Our
main task was to reflect on personal
conceptions and the use of our own
language to articulate particular and
common understandings. Doing this
kind of work was unusual for many of
the daytime laborers I encountered.
We elaborated on issues connected
to different work experiences and to
employment in general, and tried
to reach different judgments and distinctions in a variety of ways. Simple
written notes, graphs, and drawings
were made from each meeting as a
practical form of accumulating things
to be remembered, absorbed further,
and possibly expanded upon.

Duncan Campbell

b. 1972, Dublin, Ireland
lives and works in Glasgow, Scotland.

Duncan Campbell is a filmmaker
whose documentary-based works
blur the divides between record and
interpretation, historical narrative
and media representation. With
the conviction that documentary is
only "a peculiar form of fiction,"
Campbell's films, such as *Make It
New John* and *Bernadette* hold a lens
up to troubled histories with an
incisive attention to rereading.
Campbell received his MFA in 1998
from the Glasgow School of Art and
his BA in 1996 from the University
of Ulster at Belfast.

Marianne Flotron

b. 1970, Meiringen, Switzerland
lives and works in Amsterdam.

I am mainly interested in the inter-
relationship between political and
economic systems and human
behavior—how the subject creates

society and how, in turn, society creates its subjects. Recently, I have been employing different role-playing techniques and applying them to actual situations to explore the impact of social science on behavior. For *Work,* I brought the Theater of the Oppressed to the employees of a Dutch insurance company. I invited Hector Aristizábal, a Theater of the Oppressed director, to work for one week in the company. The piece focused on the influence of the capitalist system on employee mentality and revealed psychological strategies used to increase their productivity.

Paul Graham

b. 1956, United Kingdom
lives and works in New York City.

Paul Graham is a photographer credited with bringing about a revolution in British documentary approaches that embrace color, most notably in his *A1-The Great North Road* (1981–82), a series of color photographs taken along the first major road to run the entire length of England, and *Beyond Caring* (1984–85), which depicts unemployment offices throughout the country. Among more than ten other publications, *Empty Heaven* is devoted to Japan, and *A Shimmer of*

Possibility comprises twelve volumes examining the United States.

Tehching Hsieh

b. 1950, Nanjhou, Taiwan
lives and works in New York City.

I was born in 1950 in Taiwan to an atheist father and a devoted Christian mother. I dropped out of high school in 1967 and took up painting. After finishing army service (1970–73), I had my first solo show at the gallery of the American News Bureau in Taiwan and stopped painting shortly after that. In 1973 I made a perfor-mance action, *Jump Piece*, and broke both ankles. Trained as a sailor, which I used as a means to enter the United States, in July of 1974 I arrived at the port of a small town near the Delaware River in Philadelphia. I was an illegal immigrant for fourteen years until I was granted amnesty in the US in 1988.

Starting from 1978, using long durations, making art and life simultaneously, I made five *One Year Performances* and a *Thirteen-year Plan*, inside and outside my studio in New York City. Since 2000, released from the restriction of not showing my works during the *Thirteen-year Plan*, I have been exhibiting my work in North and South America, Asia, and Europe.

Richard Ibghy & Marilou Lemmens

b. 1964, Montreal
b. 1976, Lennoxville, Quebec
live and work in Montreal and Vancouver.

Our collaborative practice began in 2002 and encompasses installation, video, photography, large format wall drawings, performance, and printed matter. It combines a minimalist approach to the form and construction of the art object with a desire to make ideas visible. We like to use language's subversive potential to interrogate knowledge formations, institutional contexts, and social and psychological entanglements. A key aspect of our practice consists of bringing language to its sculptural potential, not necessarily in the sense of giving materiality to words and other communication devices, but by emphasizing the materialism of the signifier that is singular and embodied.

Over the last few years, our work has questioned the rationale upon which economic actions are described and represented, and, more generally,

how the logic of economics has come to infiltrate the most intimate areas of human life. From 2008 to 2010, we developed an umbrella project entitled *Horse and Sparrow*, which is concerned with producing visual and semantic devices that articulate a reticence towards the models, systems, and narratives put forth by economists. More recent projects explore how desire and belief influence economic discourse and practices, sustain current economies, but also carry the potential for inciting new forms of doing economy.

kleines postfordistisches Drama

(kleines postfordistisches Drama/small postfordist Drama)

kpD was based in Berlin and consisted of Brigitta Kuster, Isabell Lorey, Marion von Osten and Katja Reichard.

kpD (kleines postfordistisches Drama/ small postfordist Drama) was a group that developed in the framework of the exhibition *Atelier Europa* held in the spring of 2004 at the Kunstverein München. kpD drew attention to the social context in which cultural producers presently have to position themselves, given that they were increasingly conventionalized into role models of economic privatization and an economization of the public.

Their film, *Kamera läuft!* (2004), consists of fifteen lengthy interviews with precarious cultural producers in Berlin, based on an updated questionnaire of Italian militant employee inquiries of the 1960s. The interviews were shortened and then interpreted by actors in front of the camera in a casting in Zurich. Through the film, kpD shows that there is still the need today to change living and working conditions.

Sharon Lockhart

b. 1964, Norwood, Massachusetts, USA lives and works in Los Angeles.

My work emerges from extensive, site-specific research. Between 2007 and 2008, I spent one year in Bath, Maine, sharing the daily routines of workers at the Bath Iron Works (BIW), a steel manufacturing plant that specializes in the production of naval warcraft and is one of the last remaining factories of its kind in the USA that has not outsourced labor. My film, *Lunch Break* (2008) examines the evolving conditions of domestic American labor practice and features forty-two of the nearly 5,000 workers at BIW as they take their midday meal break— thirty minutes during the eight-hour workday that were hard fought for and remain in constant jeopardy. In an interview with fellow filmmaker James Benning (published in *Lunch Break*, 2010, edited by Sabine Eckmann), I explain that in the making the film, "I had a very hard time gaining access to BIW because of strict government security. Prior to moving to the East Coast, I spent ten months having official letters sent to management explaining who I was and what the project was about. But they said "no access" each time. It wasn't until I arrived in Bath and began to talk to people in town, who I met through family friends or friends of friends, that Local 6, the union, invited me in for a meeting. They loved the project and fought for my access." Collaboration with those I film is a matter of engaging in a mutual enterprise of representation, a social endeavor. As I described to Benning in our interview, "I find an interest, approach people whom I want to invite to participate, establish a rapport with them, and develop the project. Then there's an exchange at the end. Usually, people start out being hesitant, but also strangely intrigued. As they get to know me, I explain what I'm doing and I show them the things that are interesting to me, and they see that it could be fun to participate. It is important to me to have everyone feel that they are a part of the project...I've always made it clear that my work is about a different kind of exchange."

MTL (Nitasha Dhillon & Amin Husain)

b. 1985, Rangareddy, India
b. 1975, Chicago, USA
live and work in New York City, USA.

MTL is involved with the publication, *Tidal*, a strategic platform that explores radical possibilities created by the rupture of the Occupy movement and its aftermath.

We are MTL, a collaboration that joins research, aesthetics, and activism in its practice. MTL's underlying interest is the experience of being human and the broader cultural and social arrangements that make up our lives. As a movement, MTL attempts to describe a complete circle; its direct action is never in support of or in opposition to one side of a controversial issue. Who speaks on behalf of someone and why matters. Such interest in voice is triggered by the observation that governments no longer represent the will of the people. On the ground, MTL circumvents, filters,

and reaches unheard voices. It talks to people about life and their situation, documenting the roads and geographies that lead to conversation. Sometimes MTL is a passenger and other times a driver. It listens, witnesses, and understands. Then it reports.

Michala Paludan

b. 1980, Copenhagen, Denmark
where she lives and works.

In my work, I investigate our relationship to history and ideology. I explore how political, cultural, and scientific systems change the ways we think about the world around us, specifically, how we use imagery to represent ourselves and others in relation to how we shape our society. My starting point is often in archives, both personal and official, sifting through them to find resonances without current social conditions. I often overlay different systems of meaning production on top of each other to create a space of friction. The medium depends on the subject, and I have made slideshows, videos, and installations.

I am currently researching the worker's movements in Scandinavia, a history that is critical to the contemporary Scandinavian welfare state, but also a movement and class identity that is slowly disappearing because of changes in society and our relationship to work. The work, *Revy* (2012), considers the role of staging in protest movements. By reproducing props from a worker's theater sketch in Denmark of the 1930s, *Revy* reflects on the Occupy movement today.

Olivia Plender

b. 1977, London
lives and works in Berlin.

My research-based practice is concerned with the ideological framework around the narration of history and, more recently, changing attitudes to education and value. In 2010, I made an architectural installation, *Google Office*, for the Taipei Biennial, Taiwan. The piece questioned the commodification of knowledge and sociality within post-Fordist service-based economies, the collapse of the distinction between work and leisure, and the new identity of the entrepreneur. Use of the *Google Office* was subject to a contract whereby viewers gave up the rights to any new knowledge produced within the space, which subsequently became the intellectual property of the Taipei Biennial. Equipped with

games and free Wi-Fi, the *Google Office* was frequently occupied by people genuinely playing or working, seemingly unaware that they had become performers in the piece.

Allan Sekula

b. 1951, Erie, Pennsylvania, USA
lives and works in Los Angeles.

Allan Sekula is an American photographer, writer, critic, and filmmaker. Since the early 1970s his work has bridged the gap between conceptual art and documentary practices, focusing on economic and social themes ranging from family life, to work and unemployment, to schooling and the military-industrial complex. While calling many of the conventions of documentary into question, he continues to see photography as a social practice, answerable to the world and its problems.

Contributors

Jeanne Betak

is a graphic designer who collaborates
with artists, architects, musicians,
writers, editors and curators to
develop and produce unique contemporary publications and catalogues.
Recent publications include *A New
Nature. 9 Architectural Conditions
Between Liquid and Solid* (The Royal
Danish Academy of Fine Arts School
of Architecture Publishers, Copenhagen) and the edition *The Roads
Around* (published in cooperation
with the Rungstedlund Foundation).
She is based in Copenhagen.
www. jeannebetak.com

Will Bradley

is Artistic Director at Kunsthall Oslo,
where he produced "Arbeiderbilder"
(2012). Publications include *Art and
Social Change: A Critical Reader*
(Tate Publishing and Afterall Books,
2007), *Self Organisation/Counter-
economic Strategies* (Sternberg Press,
2007).

Cora Fisher

is a New-York based writer and
emerging curator. She earned her MA
at the Center for Curatorial Studies,
Bard College, NY, and her BFA at
the School of Art at The Cooper Union
for the Advancement of Science and
Art. She has been a staff writer for
the *Brooklyn Rail* since 2008 and has
written criticism and essays for
various publications including
Bomblog and The Rumpus. Her
recent exhibition, *Persona Ficta*,
considers performance actions that
appopriate legal procedures towards
idiosyncratic ends.

Peter Fleming

is Professor of Work and Society at
City University, London. He studies
the politics of employment today
and the emergence of new labor
movements. His recent books include
Dead Man Working (Zero Books,
2012) and *The End of Corporate
Social Responsibility* (Sage, 2013).

Milena Hoegsberg

is Acting Chief Curator at Henie
Onstad Kunstsenter (HOK). She
earned her MA at the Center for
Curatorial Studies, Bard College,
NY, and her BA in Art History at
Columbia University, with a focus on
20th century art and contemporary
time-based media. At HOK she has
curated solo shows with Omer Fast
and Ann Cathrin November Høibo.
She recently edited the publications
Omer Fast: 5000 Feet is the Best
(Sternberg Press, 2012) and *Shaped
by Time* (Revolver Publishing, 2012).

Annette Kamp

is Associate Professor PhD at the
Department for Environmental,
Social and Spatial Change at Roskilde
University, Denmark. Her main area
of research is modern working life,
in particular boundaryless work,
self-management, and temporality.
She is the author of several books
and co-editor of the *Nordic Journal
of Working Life Studies*.

Ole Martin Rønning

is Senior Archivist at the Labor
Movement Archives and Library,
Oslo. As a historian, he earned his
PhD at the University of Oslo,
specializing in the history of
Communism and the international
Communist movement.

Kathi Weeks

teaches in the Women's Studies
Program at Duke University. Her
primary interests are in the fields of
political theory, feminist theory,
Marxist thought, and utopian
studies. She is the author of
Constituting Feminist Subjects
(Cornell University Press, 1998),
*The Problem with Work: Feminism,
Marxism, Antiwork Politics
and Postwork Imaginaries* (Duke
University Press, 2011), and a
coeditor of *The Jameson Reader*
(Blackwell, 2000).

Julia Bryan-Wilson

is Associate Professor of Modern and
Contemporary Art at the University
of California, Berkeley. She is the
author of *Art Workers: Radical
Practice in the Vietnam War Era*
(University of California Press, 2009)
and the editor of *Robert Morris*
(MIT Press, October Files series,
2013).

Acknowledgements

Some of the texts in *Living Labor* have been previously published. We thank the original publishers and copyright holders for their permission to reprint.

Julia Bryan-Wilson

"Occupational Realism"

MIT Press: The Drama Review 56:4 (Winter 2012). © 2012 MIT. Republished by permission of the copyright holder and author.

Kathi Weeks

Excerpts from several chapters in *The Problem with Work*. © 2011 Duke University Press. All rights reserved. Republished by permission of the copyright holder.

Carl Cederström and Peter Fleming

"'Mainlining' Life into Dead Labor"

Dead Man Working (Winchester, UK: Zero Books, 2012). © 2012 Zero Books. Republished by permission.

Henie Onstad Kunstsenter
gratefully acknowledges the generous support of
the Freedom of Expression Foundation

FRITT ORD

LIVING
LABOR

Published by Sternberg Press

Edited by Milena Hoegsberg and Cora Fisher

Design: Jeanne Betak, Copenhagen

Copyediting: Bryne McLaughlin

Printing: Narayana, Denmark

Paper: Munken Pure; Munken Polar

Font: Serifa; Univers

—

This publication was produced in conjunction with the exhibition

ARBEIDSTID

Henie Onstad Kunstsenter (HOK), Oslo

May 23–September 1, 2013

—

ISBN 978-3-943365-67-2

Sternberg Press

Caroline Schneider

Karl-Marx-Allee 78

D-10243 Berlin

www.sternberg-press.com